A PARISH GUIDE TO ADULT INITIATION

Kenneth Boyack, C.S.P.

A PARISH GUIDE
TO ADULT INITIATION

PAULIST PRESS
New York/Ramsey

NIHIL OBSTAT
Monsignor Joseph S. Showfety
Censor Librorum

IMPRIMATUR
†Michael J. Begley
Diocese of Charlotte

July 6, 1979

Library of Congress
Catalog Card Number: 79-91001

ISBN: 0-8091-2282-0

Published by Paulist Press
Editorial Office: 1865 Broadway, New York, N.Y. 10023
Business Office: 545 Island Road, Ramsey, N.J. 07446

Printed and bound in the
United States of America

CONTENTS

*To Rev. Francis Benham
and the Christian Community of
Holy Spirit Parish, Forestville, Maryland*

INTRODUCTION

This book is a guide for those who want to make evangelization and Christian initiation come alive in the parish. Many Catholics are becoming aware of the challenge of evangelization and many have heard of the *Rite of Christian Initiation of Adults* (RCIA). This book will provide suggestions for implementing the RCIA based on a strong evangelization program.

A Parish Guide to Adult Initiation takes the reader on a journey through the various periods and stages of the RCIA. Some preparation and planning, however, are needed in order to implement the rite. After discussing this preparation in Chapter 1, we begin our journey through the RCIA itself. The second chapter on evangelization and the precatechumenate expands this period of the rite and includes some of the principles of *On Evangelization in the Modern World* by Pope Paul VI. Evangelization and Christian initiation are inseparably united. Chapters 3 through 5 give ideas and suggestions on how the catechumenate, the period of election, and the sacraments of initiation can be implemented in a parish. Chapter 6 describes postbaptismal catechesis and expands this period of the RCIA by discussing possible programs for a parish during the time from Easter to Pentecost. The final chapter gives a word of hope for continued efforts in evangelization and initiation through using the RCIA. The rite itself is referenced extensively, but not quoted directly in this book. Many reading *A Parish Guide to Adult Initiation* will want to have the RCIA as a companion volume in order to read the referenced sections in their entirety.

What this book presents, then, is a readable and practical journey through the RCIA. It not only deals with the "why" and the "how to," but also presents the feelings and reactions of people who are involved in the processes of evangelization and Christian initiation. Although the people in this book are fictitious, their experiences are real. The characters have been developed from my own pastoral experience and from my experiences of implementing the RCIA. The journey through the RCIA does bring about conversion in the minds and hearts of those involved. It is the process of conversion to Jesus Christ that makes the RCIA exciting and wonder-full.

One of the purposes of this book is to help make the RCIA the "thing to do" in every parish. The rite is too good just to be left on the shelf and not tried or experienced. "Taste and see" could be a motto for those somewhat hesitant to use the RCIA.

A Parish Guide to Adult Initiation is meant for those who want some help in tasting and seeing. I hope that pastors, members of pastoral teams, catechists, liturgists, sponsors, and members of a parish who are interested in implementing the RCIA will find this book helpful. It is meant to be a guide, to stir up ideas, and ultimately to assist those in a parish in adapting and molding the periods and stages of the RCIA to the needs and circumstances of their particular community. Each parish will have a unique journey through the RCIA, just as each person experiencing the process of evangelization and initiation will have his/her unique journey. The RCIA presents a common roadmap for both.

I am deeply grateful to those who gave me assistance in bringing this book into a readable form. Special thanks to Reverend Robert Kinast of the Catholic University of America for his lucid and critical comments. Special thanks as well to Jean Marie Hiesberger and Reverend George Fitzgerald, C.S.P., of Paulist Press for their perceptive editorial assistance. I also especially wish to thank the following people for reading and commenting on the manuscript: Reverend Thomas A. Krosnicki, S.V.D., Executive Director of the Bishops' Committee on the Liturgy; Reverend Bob Stamschror, Representative for Religious Education, United States Catholic Conference; Reverend Ben Hunt, C.S.P.; Reverend David O'Brien, C.S.P.; Reverend Ken McGuire, C.S.P.; Ms. Terra Prymuszewski; Ms. Jan Viktora; Mrs. Richard Leiden; Reverend W. Ronald Jameson; and Reverend Francis Benham. Thanks as well to Reverend John Mudd of the Archdiocesan Office of Social Development, Washington, D.C., for his comments regarding the *Rend Your Hearts* and the *Jesus Is Lord* programs. Finally, I wish to thank Mrs. Margaret Kezer for typing part of the manuscript.

Chapter One

PREPARING TO IMPLEMENT THE RCIA

The English translation of the *Rite of Christian Initiation of Adults* was published by the United States Catholic Conference in 1974. Those preparing to implement the rite in a parish will have a number of questions. Do I really want to use the rite? How will I plan for it? Who will help me? The purpose of this chapter is to answer these and other questions about implementing the RCIA.

DO I REALLY WANT TO USE THE RCIA?

To answer this question, it is instructive to look at reasons why some parishes are using the rite successfully. There are at least five reasons why the rite should be implemented in a parish community.

1. *It Builds Community.* This reason for using the RCIA cannot be stressed enough. Many of us have met interesting people because we were invited to a party, joined a singing group, or campaigned for our favorite member of Congress. These are occasions for forming relationships. The RCIA provides occasions for people to meet, build relationships, and celebrate together. The rite of becoming catechumens, for example, is an occasion for celebrating relationships that the candidate has formed with God, sponsors, catechists, and some of those present in the congregation.

2. *It Meets a Definite Need.* A number of bishops, clergy, and lay persons are becoming very interested in evangelization. This is especially true after the appearance of Pope Paul's Apostolic Exhortation, *On Evangelization in the Modern World*, which was published

in 1975. A question asked by some who are concerned about evangelization is, "What do we do with those who respond to our invitation and want to learn more about the Catholic way of life?"

The RCIA is a natural follow-up to any evangelization effort. Nos. 9–13 of the RCIA contain information on evangelization and the precatechumenate, while other sections of the Introduction, especially Nos. 1–8 and 14–40, help explain the relationship between evangelization and initiation. *On Evangelization in the Modern World* and the RCIA complement one another very well.

3. *It Creates a New Identity.* We form much of our personal identity because of what we do. If a person is married and has a family, he/she learns a new identity as a husband and father, or wife and mother. A man ordained to the priesthood learns his new identity as he carries out his pastoral responsibilities.

Catholics who attend Mass only on Sunday have a certain identity as well. Take the example of an average Catholic family. John and Kathy have two children and have been attending Mass faithfully since they registered at St. Lawrence parish four years ago. John is a good man, prays with his wife and children at home, but feels no involvement in the parish other than putting his money in the collection each week and attending an occasional meeting of the Men's Club. Kathy occasionally visits the nursing home with other women of the parish. John doesn't feel that he has any special responsibility in welcoming new members to St. Lawrence. Actually, he notices that few people at the 10:00 Mass seem to care if they know the person sitting next to them. John and Kathy's identity as Catholics is mostly tied up with their attending Mass on Sunday and trying to live a good life.

Now suppose that members of St. Lawrence parish decide to implement the RCIA and that Connie is in charge of the sponsor program. Connie knows John and Kathy; she asks them to be sponsors. "I've never heard of Catholics being sponsors for adults before," says Kathy. "I thought we only had godparents for infant baptism." Then Connie explains, "We have a number of adults who are interested in becoming Catholics. As sponsors, you would be responsible for insuring that one of these inquirers is cared for and feels welcome. We will have a couple of training sessions with other sponsors, and we can learn together what being a sponsor would involve here at St. Lawrence." "This makes a lot of sense to me," Kathy thinks to herself. "If I were becoming a Catholic, I would like a family to be my sponsor. At least I would know someone." After talking it over, John and Kathy decide to be sponsors and go to the training sessions. They become sponsors for Sandra and are very active through all the stages of the RCIA.

By being sponsors, John and Kathy form a new identity as Catholics at St. Lawrence. They feel more responsible and know that their presence does make a difference. Through getting to know Sandra, John and Kathy become more aware of the problems of people new to the Church. Now they feel more of a responsibility to greet people they do not know at the 10:00 Mass. Those St. Lawrence parishioners who work on the evangelization program, teach as catechists, or participate in the liturgical celebrations of the RCIA feel a new sense of identity as well.

4. *It Works.* With proper planning and team work, the RCIA can be implemented very successfully in almost every parish or community setting. This, of course, is presuming that members of a parish understand the rite, implement it fully, and are willing to do some work. While there have been no formal scientific studies in the United States to prove that the RCIA is successful, there is concrete experiential evidence in its favor. Parishes in Denver, Chicago, Washington, D.C., and other places across the country have in fact used the RCIA quite successfully.

5. *It is Approved by the Church.* Based on the decrees of Vatican II, the Congregation for Divine Worship prepared the new rite, and it was approved by Pope Paul VI in 1972. The text on the cover page of the 1974 English translation of the RCIA explains that it has been "approved for interim use in the Dioceses of the United States of America by the Bishops' Committee on the Liturgy and the Executive Committee of the National Conference of Catholic Bishops and confirmed by the Apostolic See."

A decision to use the RCIA involves a commitment by a parish community to a process of evangelization and initiation during the liturgical year. This process can best be carried out through a Core Group composed of clergy, parish staff, and dedicated parishioners.

A workable time frame for evangelization and initiation within a parish community can be seen in the following calendar:

June:
    Core Group plans for the RCIA

July–August:
    Planning for the evangelization program, and planning for the precatechumenate and catechumenate

September–October:
    Evangelization, and sponsor selection and training

October–November:
    Precatechumenate

November–February:
    Rite of Becoming Catechumens and catechumenate

First Sunday of Lent:
    Rite of Election and the beginning of purification and enlightenment

Third Sunday of Lent—Fourth Sunday of Lent—Fifth Sunday of Lent:
    Scrutinies

Easter Vigil:
    Sacraments of Initiation—baptism, confirmation, and eucharist

Easter—Pentecost:
    Postbaptismal catechesis

Pentecost:
    Celebrates the ending of one evangelization and initiation cycle

May—June:
    Core Group evaluates the RCIA

HOW A PARISH GOES ABOUT
IMPLEMENTING THE RCIA

If one is excited about the rite, or is fairly convinced that it is at least worth trying, the next reaction should be, "Well, let's get going!" Enthusiasm is great, but there are some prior considerations. Each parish is unique. A black urban parish will have a different situation than a predominantly white parish in the suburbs. A parish community of 300 families will have different resources and needs than a parish with 1000 families.

Regardless of the type of community, there are three steps that members of a parish might take as they implement the RCIA. The first is to gather together a "Core Group" of staff members and parishioners who would be interested in learning about the RCIA and helping to make it work in the parish. The second step is for the Core Group to plan a calendar of events that would schedule the implementation of the rite for an entire liturgical year. The third step would be to establish the different Christian service roles that are involved in making the RCIA successful in a parish. Evengelists, sponsors, catechists, liturgists, and others should become familiar with the rite, know what they are to do and when to do it.

While going through these three steps of gathering a Core Group, planning a calendar, and developing roles of Christian service is only one way of going about the task of implementing the RCIA, it is a way of making sure that the rite is adapted to meet the needs and unique character of the local parish community. Imposing the rite "from on high," without the consent or understanding of different members of the community, will bring about only confusion and perhaps resentment. On the other hand, members of a Core Group, working closely with catechists, sponsors, and others involved in the rite, can plan a process of evangelization and initiation that will meet the unique needs of that parish community.

THE CORE GROUP

The idea of getting a number of people together to get something done is not new to a parish community. We have committees for liturgy, for the parish bazaar, for planning retreat weekends, and for many other activities. Those who have been involved in a liturgy committee meeting know that on many occasions two heads are better than one. Usually each person serving on a committee contributes something and, for the most part, the group has a sense of accomplishment.

A Core Group getting together for implementing the RCIA is no different from other groups in the parish coming together to meet a need. This Core Group should be comprised of people who have agreed to give time and energy to accomplish a common goal. We know from our past experience that a priest cannot do it all, nor should he. There are many talented and willing lay persons who are needed to make the RCIA work. Lay persons are not only needed to make the rite a success, they are essential to its very vision (No. 41). Gathering a Core Group is a first step in getting parishioners involved in the RCIA.

Who Should Be in the Core Group?

In a very real sense, the rite can be thought of as a jigsaw puzzle. There are many pieces to it, and omitting some of the pieces leaves the picture incomplete. For example, implementing the rite without sponsors would be like leaving out some of the pieces in the puzzle.

Who are the people who would make good members of the Core Group? Some "most likely" members would be:

1. The pastor or some other priest from the parish staff. The primary reason for having this person involved is that without his support and enthusiasm the RCIA cannot work. Sponsors, evangelists, catechists, and others need his support and encouragement. He will be the main celebrant at the liturgies of the RCIA and will need to carry out other pastoral duties listed in No. 45 of the rite. He may be needed as well to answer some of the theological questions that come up in the discussions.

2. A coordinator of the evangelization programs. Since most of our parishes do not have a history of strong evangelization, getting someone who is interested may be all that can be expected at the beginning. We have talked about the need to see evangelization and initiation as two aspects of one effort. Having a person in the Core Group committed to evangelization helps the group to focus on evangelization as called for within the RCIA.

3. A coordinator of the sponsor program. The role of sponsor, described in Nos. 42–43 of the RCIA, is somewhat unfamiliar; again, the person/s selected might have only an interest. Skill and expertise can be gained through experience. The sponsor program involves selection, training, and the continuing pastoral care of sponsors.

4. The Director of Religious Education or someone knowledgeable in the catechetical area. The office of catechist is described in No. 48 of the rite. Not only does the catechist have the job of developing a curriculum in line with the vision of the rite, but of coordinating and planning with the pastor, sponsors, and those involved in the initiation liturgies.

5. A coordinator of activities involving both the candidates and the community. The Core Group should meet the challenge of No. 4 of the rite and involve parishioners in the initiation of the candidates. Examples of this type of involvement might be for the members of the parish council to meet with the candidates on a Sunday morning during the catechumenate, or for the members of the community and the candidates to meet in prayer groups during Lent. Someone is needed to coordinate these activities and see that they best meet the needs of the particular parish.

6. A coordinator of publicity. The RCIA is new to most members of the parish and must be explained. A person coordinating publicity would see that announcements, posters, prepared articles, etc., keep everyone informed.

7. Parish discerners. Perhaps one or two people from the parish could attend the meetings of the Core Group, but not have responsibility for coordinating any activities. Their job is just to listen and tell the Core Group whether or not their decisions make sense to the average parishioner.

8. The parish liturgist or someone from the parish liturgy committee. The liturgical celebrations are vital to the success of the rite. These liturgies involve not only the candidates, but sponsors, catechists, the celebrant, and the entire community. Having a liturgist as a member of the Core Group can be very helpful for liturgy planning, as well as for insuring that these celebrations capture the "mood" of the community.

9. A general coordinator. This person is needed to lead the

11

Core Group meetings and be responsible for the overall implementation of the RCIA in the parish.

The roles and duties of these Core Group members will be discussed more fully later on in this chapter.

Some parishes may choose to include all of the above as members of their Core Group. Others may decide that fewer persons are needed. Regardless of the actual number, however, all of the tasks mentioned in items 1 to 9 above should be considered when a Core Group is implementing the RCIA. Having more people rather than fewer reduces the amount of work done by any one person and can increase team support.

The pastor or whoever is selecting the Core Group members should make it a high priority to get good people. The RCIA can make a real impact on the parish, and the Core Group members will have a definite influence on whether this impact is positive or negative. Try to get people for the Core Group who are committed Christians, who have leadership potential, and who demonstrate a willingness and ability to serve.

Working Together

Once Core Group members have been selected and have agreed to serve in this ministry, the next challenge is for them to become familiar with the RCIA and learn to work together.

The challenge of becoming familiar with the rite will be met differently by different Core Groups. However, here are some training suggestions that apply quite generally:

1. Read the Introduction to the RCIA and discuss it as a group.

2. Read and discuss *A Parish Guide to Adult Initiation.*

3. Read and talk about selections from *Made, Not Born, New Perspectives on Christian Initiation and the Catechumenate* (Notre Dame,Ind.: University of Notre Dame Press, 1976). This is a collection of articles concerning the history of Christian initiation and current theologizing on the rite. Chapters 1, 6, 7, and 8 are especially helpful.

4. Read and discuss the *National Bulletin on Liturgy,* Vol. 11, No. 64 (May–June 1978). Entitled "Christian Initiation: Into Full Communion," this volume has a complete discussion of the RCIA

and suggests items for further reading. The *National Bulletin on Liturgy* is a review published by the Canadian Conference of Catholic Bishops and is available from Publications Service, 90 Parent Avenue, Ottawa, Ontario, Canada K1N7B1.

5. Read and become familiar with *Becoming a Catholic Christian* (New York: William H. Sadlier, Inc., 1978). This is a collection of articles on the RCIA presented at an international symposium in France. Many aspects of the rite are treated in detail.

6. Discuss the importance of a supporting Christian community and how this type of community can be nourished and fostered. Stephen B. Clark's book *Building Christian Communities* (Notre Dame, Ind.: Ave Maria Press, 1972) provides helpful ideas for discussion.

7. Take an evening or a Saturday to role play the rite of becoming catechumens or some other liturgical rite. Take time to develop a prayerful mood. Discuss the feelings and attitudes of each person playing a role. It is important that the Core Group experience itself as a supporting Christian community.

8. Do a "brainstorming" exercise on how the parish might be different if strong evangelization and initiation programs were carried out. See if there is a consensus among group members concerning the vision of the rite. Conclude this exercise with shared prayer.

A Core Group with a basic understanding of the areas covered by items 1 to 8 above will be well enough prepared and committed to begin implementing the rite. Group members should not short-change the group by skipping this training phase.

The Core Group is truly that, a *group* of people who work together and are committed to one another. Sometimes people find groups inefficient and a cause of much frustration. But this need not be the case. Many problems will be avoided if group members make good decisions about how they will work together. Here are some areas to consider:

1. Is there an atmosphere of acceptance and trust in the group? Or do people feel threatened and clam up?

2. Are group members encouraged to make their assumptions clear? Perhaps the group coordinator occasionally could ask members to state their assumptions. One example would be talking about the value of evangelization for the parish.

3. Are group members encouraged to talk about their motivation? Edward, for example, was asked to be on the Core Group, but agreed only because the pastor asked him. After a couple of training sessions Edward became excited about the vision of the rite and became more committed to making the rite work. When Edward shares his change of motivation with the Core Group, he helps the others know him better and realize his increased commitment.

4. Are members encouraged to communicate openly and freely during the meeting? Or is there more honest communication in the parking lot after the meeting is over? Group members should feel free to share their feelings of frustration, anxiety, joy, or exhilaration. Feeling free enough to express one's opinions is also important. If a group member feels that one type of evangelization program just doesn't make sense for the parish, he/she should be encouraged to say so in the group and then see if others agree or disagree.

5. Are group members encouraged to share their experience of how the work they do in implementing the RCIA is connected to their private and parish prayer life?

The way the Core Group works together will in most cases be an indication of how they will work with the new members coming into the Church. If there is generosity, love, acceptance, trust, and authentic communication in the group, these attributes will be found in relationships with new members. If group members feel clammed up, tense, and frustrated, these feelings will be reflected.

One way for the Core Group to ensure that they are working together effectively is to spend the last ten minutes of each meeting talking about "how things have gone." During this time, the group coordinator could ask: Did you feel as though someone dominated the conversation at the expense of another member? Did you feel free to express feelings or did you hold them back? Were you satisfied with the progress of the meeting? and so on. The purpose of this ten-minute period is to encourage group members to express any unfinished business and to provide useful feedback for following meetings.

Core Group members will gain more confidence in implementing the rite as they actually experience it in progress. They will also learn to work together as a group as they continue to be open and honest in their communication.

The Core Group's Task

After Core Group members feel they are adequately trained and feel comfortable working together as a group, they can begin their work of implementing the rite. Making the RCIA successful in a parish involves (1) planning and (2) evaluation.

Planning

One way of planning is for the Core Group to meet in early June and plan the "calendar of events" for the entire year. The suggestions given in Nos. 49–57 of the RCIA present guidelines for the key dates which should appear on this calendar. No. 49 states that the sacraments of initiation—baptism, confirmation, and eucharist—should be celebrated on the Easter Vigil, which is the focal point of the entire evangelization and initiation process. The rite of election should be celebrated on the First Sunday of Lent (No. 51), and the scrutinies on the Third, Fourth, and Fifth Sundays of Lent (No. 52). The presentation of the creed is celebrated during the week after the first scrutiny, and the presentation of the Lord's Prayer occurs during the week after the third scrutiny (No. 53). There should be a period of prayer and the celebration of preparatory rites before the Easter Vigil on Holy Saturday (No. 54). After the Vigil, a Mass for the new Catholics is celebrated each Sunday until Pentecost (No. 57).

Many of these terms and rites may seem confusing since we are not familiar with them. For example, scrutiny (Nos. 154–180) is a term used to describe a liturgical rite which takes place during Mass on the Third, Fourth, and Fifth Sundays of Lent. The three scrutinies are designed to help those preparing for baptism to purify their intentions, develop a deeper relationship with Jesus, and make firmer decisions to live the Christian way of life in the parish community. The meaning of other terms and rites will become more clear as we discuss the periods and stages of the rite in Chapters 2 to 5 of this book. A certain amount of confidence is needed to accept the suggestions of the RCIA regarding when rites should be celebrated. The scrutinies, presentations, and other rites can be very rich experiences of the Church at prayer during these prescribed times of the liturgical year.

While Core Group members are expected to use pastoral sensitivity in determining how each of the rites may best meet the needs of the parish, the best general rule of thumb is to mark one's calendar in line with what the rite suggests, especially if the parish is implementing the RCIA for the first time. In other words, try the rite at face value and celebrate *all* the scrutinies, presentations, etc., at the times given in the RCIA. Doing the entire RCIA for one year will give a solid basis for evaluation. Perhaps the Core Group may find that the rite should be adapted differently next year.

What are the best times for having the period of evangelization and precatechumenate as well as the catechumenate itself? The process of arriving at dates for these periods involves "counting backwards" from the date when the rite of election is celebrated, namely, the First Sunday of Lent. The catechumenate should be long enough so that a candidate begins to live and understand the Catholic way of life during that time (No. 19). Naturally, learning this way of life will differ with each catechumen. As a general principle, however, the catechumenate could begin around early November. The day after Labor Day in September might be a practical time to begin a parish-wide evangelization program which would be followed by a precatechumenate program from October through early November.

A basic principle in planning the calendar is that there should be a complete "cycle" of the rite each year. Just as we celebrate the entire liturgical cycle each year, we are invited to celebrate the different phases of the RCIA annually. There is, then, a certain rhythm that should enter into the Core Group's planning. The group could begin to plan for the rite in early June. July and August could be rather light, except for the planning of the evangelization program for September, and some preparation by those who are catechists and liturgists. Sponsors could be selected and trained in conjunction with the evangelization program so that they are available during the precatechumenate in October. November through the First Sunday of Lent would be the time for the catechumenate, and Lent would be the period of purification and enlightenment. The sacraments of initiation are celebrated during the Easter Vigil, and the period from Easter to Pentecost is always for postbaptismal catechesis. This brings us back, full circle, to the time after Pentecost when the Core

Group, after evaluating, will begin the process of implementing the complete RCIA for another year.

A Core Group's "master calendar" might, then, look something like this for implementing the RCIA in a parish for one year:

June:
Core Group plans for the RCIA

July–August:
Planning for the evangelization program, and planning for the precatechumenate and catechumenate

September–October:
Evangelization, and sponsor selection and training

October–November:
Precatechumenate

November–February:
Rite of Becoming Catechumens and catechumenate

First Sunday of Lent:
Rite of Election and the beginning of purification and enlightenment

Third Sunday of Lent—Fourth Sunday of Lent—Fifth Sunday of Lent:
Scrutinies

Easter Vigil:
Sacraments of Initiation—baptism, confirmation, and eucharist

Easter—Pentecost:
Postbaptismal catechesis

Pentecost:
Celebrates the ending of one evangelization and initiation cycle

May–June:
    Core Group evaluates the RCIA & BEGINS A NEW CYCLE

One objection to this annual cycle is that the unique lives and experiences of people do not always fit into preconceived packages. A catechumen may not be ready or really want to become one of the "elect" on the First Sunday of Lent. However, one accommodation could be for a person choosing not to become one of the "elect" this year to celebrate the rite of election with other catechumens the next year. Such a person, then, would be a catechumen for about a year and a half, and be on a two-year cycle.

It is clear from the above that we are saying that generally a yearly cycle of the RCIA will be the best for most parishes. This cycle has the advantage of creating a consistency in the minds of parishioners. After a while the attitude will develop that "This is what we do here every year." Also, beginning the evangelization program after Labor Day has the practical advantage of insuring that most parishioners are back from summer vacation. People are generally more willing to get involved after the summer is over and school starts again. A further advantage of planning the RCIA each year in early June is that the activities of the rite can be integrated with other parish functions. Some parishes do their "yearly planning" during this time, and the key calendar events of the RCIA could be entered on the general calendar of the parish. However, depending on the situation, and especially after a year or two of using the rite, a parish may choose a two- or three-year cycle.

Once the Core Group members have marked key dates on their calendars and know generally when each phase of the RCIA will be held, more of the details can be filled in. For example, the person in charge of sponsors will need to determine when he/she will begin selecting and training sponsors for the "sponsor pool." The group may decide that it would be best to make an appeal for sponsors during a later phase of the evangelization program in order that trained sponsors are available during the precatechumenate.

As the Core Group is filling in the details of its calendar, they may want to decide on some of the following:

1. How often should the group meet to plan, pray, reflect, or simply be together?

18

2. How can the RCIA be publicized so parishioners become familiar and comfortable with it? Should there be a special time in August marked on the calendar to publicize the evangelization and initiation programs?

3. What Mass will the Core Group choose to be the focal Mass for those being initiated? Having all the rites at the 10:00 Mass on Sunday, for example, will help those who usually attend to become familiar with the sequence of the rites and get to know those being initiated.

4. How often will the candidates be personally interviewed in order to give them the best pastoral care? One suggestion would be the following four times: before the catechumenate, before the rite of election, before the sacraments of initiation, and before Pentecost. These particular times are important because they are decision points for the candidates and the faith community. The interview times should be entered on the calendar. Times for shared prayer or retreats which would precede these decision points could also be entered on the calendar.

5. How early does the Bishop need to be contacted in order to insure that he or his delegate is available to celebrate the rite of election on the First Sunday of Lent (No. 44)?

6. If the parish has used the RCIA before, does the Core Group want to plan for an anniversary celebration of those previously initiated? Since the Easter Vigil is the time to renew baptismal promises, a party or reception after the Vigil may be appropriate.

These six items are examples of the types of things that the Core Group should consider as they are planning for the RCIA. More areas for individual and group decision will become known as each member carries out his/her task of planning and adapting the rite.

Core Group members should keep in mind that not everything will be crystal-clear, especially during the first year of implementing the rite. Some activities will have to be "played by ear" and "muddled through." A good sense of humor will help.

Evaluation

The final task of the Core Group is evaluation. It would be best for the group to set its own standards and evaluation criteria, primarily because of the uniqueness of each parish. The group may wish to evaluate each activity of the evangelization and initiation process as it occurs and then take a longer period of time for evaluation after Pentecost.

Evaluating each activity is especially important the first year the RCIA is used. One example is the evaluation of the first scrutiny. Since most parishioners have not participated in a scrutiny before, it is difficult to have a good liturgical sense of how the community could really celebrate this very important time in Lent. Evaluating the first scrutiny after experiencing this celebration still allows time to change or adapt in preparation for the remaining two scrutinies.

The Core Group may find the time after Pentecost to be well suited for a major evaluation of the parish's evangelization and initiation process. The results of questionnaires or interviews used for evaluation could be utilized. Comments could be sought from those initiated, from sponsors, and from community members. Sound reflection on how it went this year will be extremely valuable in making decisions regarding evangelization and initiation programs for the coming year.

MINISTRIES, OFFICES, AND ROLES OF CHRISTIAN SERVICE IN THE RCIA

If the Core Group has planned the calendar and adapted their planning to the "mood" of the parish, the next step in implementing the rite is to develop the various ministries, offices, and roles of Christian service. The RCIA (No. 41) assumes that the baptized members of a faith community have definite roles to play in the evangelization and initiation of new members. Nos. 42–48 of the rite describe many of these roles and present the duties involved. We shall discuss some of the more important ministries, offices, and roles of Christian service in the remaining pages of this chapter.

THE EVANGELIZER

If the parish community is going to evangelize (No. 9), it needs evangelizers. Since the Roman Catholic Church has not had as much of a recent tradition in evangelization as some other Christian groups have had, those in the parish directly responsible for this area will have a challenging task that demands creativity. Many of us are stuck with bad images of "evangelizers" who knock incessantly on doors and try to "convert" residents on the spot. Not surprisingly, some Catholics have misconceptions about evangelization, and do not want to be associated with any evangelization effort. Perhaps the best way to do effective outreach in a parish would be for the coordinator of evangelization to form a team and find programs that not only fit the "mood" of the parish, but create a positive image for the evangelizer. Chapter 2 of this book should give this team a good foundation to carry on their work.

Members of a parish community should always keep in mind the connection between evangelization and initiation. As the RCIA recycles each year, and evangelization programs recur year after year, parishioners will be able to develop the attitude that evangelization is always followed up by other periods and stages of the RCIA.

THE SPONSOR

The role of sponsor (or godparent) is presented in two paragraphs within the RCIA—Nos. 42 and 43. The Roman Catholic Church has a strong tradition of having sponsors for those confirmed and godparents for infants who are baptized. We should not have too much difficulty in expanding this tradition to include sponsors or godparents for adults being initiated into the Church.

If the size of the parish is large, a sponsor team may be the best way to get a sponsor program off to a solid start. This team could be composed of the sponsor coordinator from the Core Group together with others from the parish. Working closely with the pastor, the team would work out procedures for the selection, training, and follow-up support of sponsors.

Selection of Sponsors

A parish that has 15 inquirers interested in joining the community will need 15 individuals or families to act as sponsors. The sponsor team may know potential sponsors or they may be able to get recommendations from members of the Core Group or other parish organizations.

After potential sponsors have been selected, a meeting should be held in which the general expectations for the sponsors are stated. Being a sponsor requires a formal commitment to a candidate from the time of the precatechumenate through Pentecost. Once the expectations are given, individuals will be able to decide if they have the time and desire to continue with the sponsor training program.

It is important to realize that the actual sponsors for inquirers cannot be assigned until the inquiring candidates have gathered in the precatechumenate period. Some inquirers may know friends or relatives from the parish community whom they would want as sponsors and who would be qualified for this role. If that is the case, these personally chosen sponsors will require training.

Sponsor Training

Training sessions for the sponsors will vary with each parish. Regardless of the parish setting, one of the main goals of the training will be to instill the attitude that sponsors are not expected to be theological experts, but rather friends who are living the Christian way of life and wish to accompany an inquirer on his/her journey. Sponsors can do more by a caring relationship than by being "people who know all the answers."

Sponsors can be given materials to read, such as chapters from this book, which will help them learn about their role and the important part they play in the overall process of the RCIA. One way of helping these parishioners to get the "feel" of being a sponsor is to do role playing. Take turns at role playing the situation when the sponsor and inquirer initially meet; or role play a situation in which the inquirer is very frustrated and is thinking strongly about not coming any more. Talk about thoughts and feelings in these situations.

Sponsors who attend the training sessions should be encouraged to share their past experiences about how they felt welcome in an organization and what others did to make them feel that way. Time should also be taken for the sponsors to share prayer in a liturgical setting.

The sponsors will likely come up with some good suggestions to help make the sponsor program a success. These people can take a great amount of personal responsibility for their own training, and for actually developing the office of sponsor.

Sponsors should be told that there will be some difficulties along the way and that not every sponsor-candidate relationship will be successful. They should know, too, that there is ongoing training and pastoral support available to them. Portions of these follow-up training meetings could be set aside for sponsors to reflect on their own experiences and help one another to deal with mutual problems, or to share approaches and activities that have worked well.

Matching the Sponsor with the Inquirer

The process of matching trained sponsors with inquirers takes place during the precatechumenate. Care should be taken to match age levels, interests, and other factors that may contribute to a meaningful relationship between the sponsor and inquirer. A single adult may be very good for another single adult or, perhaps, a family could sponsor another family.

After the sponsors have been matched up with the inquirers, team members can inform the larger parish community about who will represent them in the office of sponsor. There could be a short commissioning ceremony, announcements at the Masses, or pictures of the sponsors in the back of the church. The sponsor team could also choose to have an appreciation dinner for the sponsors and their families.

It should be noted here that even though most of the sponsors will be assigned during the precatechumenate period in the fall, members of the "sponsor pool" may be called on to serve at other times. For example, the pastor may meet someone during Lent who is interested in becoming a Catholic. He may feel that it is best for the person to go through the precatechumenate and catechumenate period in the fall. Meanwhile, a sponsor could be assigned to this person and meet with him/her at least once a month. This sponsor-inquirer relationship could continue when the person becomes a catechumen in the fall.

The Role of the Sponsor

The selection, training, and pastoral support for the sponsor revolves around what the sponsor actually does in that role. The RCIA describes many of the sponsor duties in Nos. 19.2, 19.4, 42, 43, and 104. Since we have little experience of having adult sponsors for adult candidates, we can best understand what is involved by looking at (1) the relationship of the sponsor to the candidate, (2) the relationship of the sponsor to the parish staff, (3) the sponsor's personal responsibility, and (4) the candidate's relationship with the sponsor.

1. The Relationship of the Sponsor to the Candidate
   In order to build a caring sponsor-candidate relationship, the sponsor could:
   - accompany the candidate to liturgical celebrations.
   - participate with the candidate in the catechumenate, such as occasionally attending classes or discussing the material presented.
   - introduce the candidate to persons in various ministries in the parish.
   - participate with the candidate in Christian service; for example, visit a nursing home on Sunday afternoons.
   - invite the candidate to dinner or go to other social events.
   - keep in phone contact.
   - offer the candidate a ride.
   - discuss the questions of doctrine.
   - pray with the candidate.
   - participate in a Scripture study with the candidate, or the sponsor and the candidate could both be in a Scripture study group.
   - listen and share the candidate's journey as he/she experiences the process of initiation.
   - invite the candidate to Catholic or Christian functions outside of the parish.
   - talk with the candidate at certain decision points in the initiation process, for example, before the person becomes a catechumen.
   - introduce the candidate to other members of the parish.
   - share Christian books or tapes.
   - share his/her own journey of faith.
   - encourage the candidate if his/her motivation is low.

2. The Relationship of the Sponsor to the Parish Staff
   Among other things, the sponsor could:
   - discuss problems or questions with the parish staff concerning the sponsor-candidate relationship.

- seek counsel.
- pray for the staff members.
- provide input for catechumenate classes.
- participate in liturgies and other functions of the RCIA.
- suggest names of potential sponsors.
- critique the sponsor training program.

3. The Sponsor's Personal Responsibility
   On his/her own initiative, the sponsor could:
   - share experiences with other sponsors.
   - become familiar with the process of the RCIA.
   - continue to deepen one's own faith life.
   - accept feelings of doubt, inadequacy, or hesitation, and share these feelings with others.

4. The Candidate's Relationship with the Sponsor
   The sponsor should be aware of some of the possible feelings of the candidate toward the sponsor. He/she should be aware that the candidate may:
   - be fearful of "bothering" the sponsor.
   - have feelings of unworthiness.
   - wish to share fears about being in a new place or meeting new people.
   - wish to share the excitement of peak experiences during the RCIA.
   - be reluctant to share on a deeply personal level.
   - be very open to a relationship of love, concern, and trust.

Carrying out the duties of a sponsor can be a growth experience. "I thank my Father in heaven that I was chosen to be a sponsor," said one man after the Easter Vigil. Many sponsors renew their own faith, learn more about Catholicism, and become friends with other sponsors and candidates during the period of initiation. Sponsors begin to realize that they are needed in a parish. After the RCIA has been implemented in a parish over a number of years, there seems a good possibility that the role of sponsor will become well known and popular.

THE CATECHIST

The duties of the catechist are presented in No. 48 of the RCIA. Catechists are not new in the Catholic Church. We have had a strong tradition of religious educators, whereas we do not have a tradition of parishioners being evangelizers. Most of us know CCD teachers, administrators, and class assistants whom we see around the church or parish hall on Sunday morning.

The office of catechist within the RCIA, however, is somewhat different from our past tradition in religious education. Catechists are involved in teaching and celebrating a new way of life. Nos. 19.1, 109, 119, 120, 130, and 143 of the RCIA speak about this. The catechist must relate to adult people who are looking for new meaning and a new way of life as Catholics. The challenge to the catechist is to respond to these adult needs within the periods and stages of the initiation process. A catechist should be interested in how adults learn and what are the best methods to help learning occur. Small groups that allow candidates to reflect on their own experiences are important. Helping adults to participate fully in liturgical celebrations or to discover how the teachings of the Catholic tradition can add meaning to their lives are all challenges for the catechist.

Perhaps the best way to meet these challenges is to form a team, with the catechist from the Core Group being one of the members. More than one catechist will be needed if there are many candidates and the team decides to have small groups. Each small group should have a catechist as a leader. The team could strongly consider having one or two candidates as members. This would be a definite help in determining if the catechists were meeting the needs of the candidates, as well as giving the candidates a chance to contribute some input and take responsibility for their own learning.

Catechists could reflect on the fact that they teach with their lives. The difference between theory and practice becomes rather obvious to someone in the class who hears a catechist talk about Christian joy and yet appears gloomy and depressed. On the other hand, there is no one more effective than a catechist who is authentically "converted" and is convinced that the Christian life is worth living and sharing with others.

THE LITURGIST

The office of liturgist is not listed among the others in Nos. 41–48. This is because the RCIA itself is like a prayer book to those who are responsible for liturgical rites. The rite of becoming catechumens, the rite of election, and other rites are all rather detailed in the RCIA so that those responsible for liturgy in the parish can best use them to celebrate the different stages of Christian initiation.

The liturgical rites are extremely important, as Nos. 19.3, 106, and 108 demonstrate. The rites are designed to help candidates express what they are feeling and thinking. The rite of becoming catechumens, for example, celebrates the inquirers' decision to come into the Church and the parishioners' joy because of receiving new members. Candidates also learn from experiencing liturgical rites. They are normally not familiar with the rich and prayerful liturgies of the Catholic Church. The celebrations of the various rites within the RCIA are learning opportunities for the candidates and the community. Liturgical rites, as well, give fond memories of life in the parish. "I will never forget how happy I was giving the sign of peace for the first time after I was baptized," said one new Catholic. Having memories that the candidates and the community can cherish is one of the gifts of the RCIA.

Celebrating liturgy well takes time, prayer, and an understanding of the "pulse" of the congregation. The task of the liturgy team is to plan good liturgies. The liturgist from the Core Group could be on this team, as well as the celebrant, musicians, and one of the candidates. This latter person could represent the other candidates and gain experience in liturgy planning. Some liturgy teams may also wish to get input from sponsors since they are involved in some of the rites.

The liturgy team should try to adapt the rites (see No. 67) so they will be celebrations for the entire community—candidates and parishioners. For example, a team may consider whether a cross or a medal should be presented to the candidates during the rite of becoming catechumens (No. 89). Each liturgy of the RCIA will present a unique challenge to the members of the team.

THE COORDINATOR OF PUBLICITY

While not listed in the RCIA, this role is important. Because the activities of the rite will be new to most parishioners, they will feel more like participating if they know what is going on. There is nothing more frustrating to some parishioners than to attend a liturgy and then have something "popped" on them without adequate preparation or explanation. This type of thing could happen with any of the rites of the RCIA. On the positive side, publicity that is well planned and sensitive to the "pulse" of the community can be very effective in helping parishioners and candidates understand and participate in the RCIA.

The person on the Core Group coordinating publicity may wish to get others to help. The team would make it their business to insure that all concerned parties know in advance the activities of the RCIA.

Here are some suggestions that may be helpful. The publicity team could:

- plan for a time in late August to explain how evangelization and initiation will be carried out in the parish during the year.
- plan publicity for each phase of the RCIA, from evangelization through the postbaptismal catechesis.
- insure that the entire community knows about the rites, and not just those who are coming to the particular Mass when the rite is being celebrated. This action will prevent people from feeling excluded or left out.
- speak to different parish organizations and inform them about the RCIA.
- decide on what media to use, and what symbols will best communicate the message. Some parishes have made large banners to hang in the church expressing the theme of the evangelization program.
- plan for press releases to local papers, radio, and television. This may be especially important if the evangelization program will go beyond parish boundaries, or if the parish is the first to use the RCIA in the area.

- take color slides of evangelization and initiation events and use these to tell people about the program next year.
- take pictures of the candidates during the year and present the new Catholics with a "pictorial history" at the final initiation ceremony at Pentecost.
- take pictures at the rites and put them in the back of the church for all to see. This is helpful for creating conversation in the vestibule after Mass.
- invite priests and parishioners from other churches to some of the liturgical celebrations of the RCIA. Some may not have participated in these types of celebrations. Having people from outside the parish gives a very real sense of the universal dimension of the Catholic Church.
- keep records for historical purposes.

THE CANDIDATE-COMMUNITY LIAISON

The role of this liaison person is intentionally vague, but the idea behind it is sound. If those who are being initiated are to learn a new way of life as Catholics, they can be helped immensely in this process by getting to know active Catholics. The candidate-community liaison can seek ways for members of the community to come into contact with the candidates. Here are some things the liaison person might do:

- have a program each Sunday during the catechumenate where active parishioners come and get to know the candidates, and vice versa. (See Chapter 3 for details.)
- seek ways of inviting interested candidates to become members of Bible study groups, prayer groups, or social action groups in the parish.
- invite candidates to Marriage Encounter, Cursillo, or other retreat activities.
- become aware of Lenten programs for the parish in which candidates can participate with other members of the parish. (For one example, see Chapter 4.)
- help new Catholics become aware of, and involved in, a form of Christian service such as lector, evangelizer, or visitor to the sick.

The liaison person should be a member of the Core Group. He/she may get others to help, especially from among the candidates. Core Group members can add ideas and discernment as to what types of activities could best foster the candidates' entry into the life of the parish community.

THE PRIEST AND DEACON

The various duties of these ordained ministries are described in Nos. 45 and 47. The duties are pastoral, catechetical, and liturgical. Little needs to be said about these ministries except that the RCIA will not be successful without the support of the clergy. Priests and deacons can help create an atmosphere for the prayerful celebration of the rites. Clergy can minister by teaching or by being pastorally present during the catechumenate classes. The parish pastor and his staff can be models of commitment and enthusiasm in evangelization and initiation.

THE COMMUNITY

We have said that initiation of the catechumens should take place in the midst of the community (No. 4). We also have referred to No. 41 of the rite and mentioned that evangelization and initiation should be the concern and responsibility of all the baptized. Saying that the "community" is responsible for evangelization and Christian initiation may seem vague. However, if the Core Group and those involved in the ministries, offices, and roles of Christian service carry out their particular duties, the "community" will not remain a vague abstraction, but will become a living reality for those who are evangelized and initiated. The "community" will indeed welcome, teach, celebrate, and minister.

Chapter Two

EVANGELIZATION AND THE PRECATECHUMENATE

We will now begin our journey through the RCIA itself. According to Nos. 6–7, there are three stages and four periods as a candidate travels toward full initiation into the Church. The roadmap for the candidate's journey looks like this:

Evangelization and precatechumenate	period 1
Rite of becoming catechumens	stage 1
Catechumenate	period 2
Rite of election (First Sunday of Lent)	stage 2
Illumination (during Lent)	period 3
Sacraments of initiation (Easter Vigil)	stage 3
Postbaptismal catechesis (Easter-Pentecost)	period 4

As we follow this roadmap making our journey through the rite, we will be interested in two areas: (1) the principles or guidelines given in the rite for the periods and stages, and (2) some practical ways in which the rite can be implemented in a parish. Before we proceed, however, the reader may wish to review the calendar on page 8 in order to understand a possible time frame during which these periods and stages of the rite can be carried out within a parish community.

EVANGELIZATION AND PRECATECHUMENATE WITHIN THE RCIA

The RCIA speaks about spiritual journeys of adults (Nos. 5–6). A person who is interested in learning more about the Catholic way of life will begin the journey by asking questions, or inquiring, about how the Church could meet his/her adult faith needs. The Church's response to this inquiry is evangelization (No. 7a). Evangelization is a proclamation of the good news that salvation for all people is found in the person of Jesus Christ. The dialogue of the inquiring person and the "good news" community takes place in a period that the Church has labeled "precatechumenate." If the unbaptized, inquiring person becomes converted to the Lord and is drawn toward the lifestyle of the Christian community, the next step will be for that person to become a catechumen. The jouney will continue until, we hope, the person becomes fully initiated into the Christian community through receiving the sacraments of baptism, confirmation, and the eucharist during the Easter Vigil.

Within the vision of the RCIA the period of evangelization and precatechumenate is very important and normally should be included when a parish is implementing the rite (No. 9). However, this period is not developed in the RCIA text. The catechumenate is the first period to be presented in detail. The implication is that the members of a parish will have to take primary responsibility for developing the evangelization and precatechumenate period of the rite.

A community committed to doing evangelization and the precatechumenate can get a good start by looking at the two general guidelines within the rite. The community should then develop its own programs within these guidelines. The first guideline is that evangelization is the responsibility of all baptized members of the community (No. 41.1). Parishoners can carry out this responsibility by talking with the candidates, inviting them to parish gatherings, and getting to know them on a social basis (No. 41.1). These are ways in which the community evangelizes. The second guideline concerns the goal of evangelization: The inquirer should experience an initial conversion to Jesus and begin to develop an adult faith during the precatechumenate period (No. 10). Different members of the community, such as catechists, deacons, priests, and lay people, should help the inquirers understand the meaning of the gospel and assist them in the conversion process (No. 11).

These guidelines are helpful because they offer a framework for the period of evangelization and precatechumenate, which is the foundation for the remaining stages of the RCIA. The precatechumenate is so important because without the "pre," in many cases, there would be no catechumenate.

Our goal for the remainder of this chapter will be to take these guidelines of the RCIA and show in more detail what evangelization and the precatechumenate could look like in parishes. We shall do this by asking how a parish community evangelizes or reaches out (in the sense of No. 41.1, our first guideline). Then, once individuals have responded to the invitations, we shall see how the community helps these inquirers attain faith and conversion to Jesus during the precatechumenate period (in the sense of Nos. 10–11, our second guideline).

REACHING OUT

There are all types of people "out there" who need the healing love of Jesus Christ.

Carl has not attended church for years, not since he went to the services run by the chaplain on post during the war. Life was fairly good for Carl until three years ago when his wife died of cancer. They had been married for 25 years and were very close. Patricia's death left a hole in Carl's heart as big as the Grand Canyon. He feels the emptiness and pain of her loss. He is lonely. . . .

Adam is young and energetic. He finished college three years ago and now works for a small corporation. Adam has always aimed at success, even when he was little. He has worked hard for his promotions and puts in a lot of overtime. Adam hasn't attended church in three years. After all, what does church have to do with achieving success? Recently, though, Adam has been getting tired of stepping on people in order to "get ahead." "There must be more to life than this," he has thought to himself. . . .

Carl and Adam are within your parish boundaries—or others

like them. People who are looking for meaning. People who seek an answer to the blistering questions of human loneliness and pain. There are men and women in your parish who are looking for the fullness of life, but have not considered looking for that life in Jesus Christ.

While there are exceptions, Catholics do not have a very good track record of reaching out for these people. Par ies have not been known as "evangelizing" communities. A recent study of three parishes in suburban Maryland showed that a substantial majority of Catholics surveyed favored trying to build up their existing parish community rather than reaching out to attract new members. (Survey data are found in *The St. Bernadette's Evangelism Experiment* [Washington, D.C.: The Paulist Office for Evangelization, 1977, p. 46].) In these three parishes Catholics were more interested in housecleaning than having guests.

Why Catholics are not more committed "evangelizers" is a puzzle. We have the command from Jesus to go and make disciples of all nations (Matt 28:10), and we know that there are many "out there" who are looking for meaning and for a fullness of life which the gospel can give.

The very program we are talking about has proved a partial, practical solution to the problem. Implementing the RCIA has raised consciousness in some communities concerning the importance of evangelization itself. Reaching out to the "unchurched"—non-baptized persons, baptized non-Catholics who have no church affiliation, and inactive Catholics—begins to take on a value when members of a community realize what a difference their love and concern can make to those who feel alienated. A Catholic who has cared about an unchurched person, and eventually sees this person find meaning and a new life in the Catholic community, cannot but feel more convinced of the value of reaching out to others.

One of the better ways to develop community evangelization is to have certain types of outreach each year, as the parish is implementing the RCIA. Each September, for example, parishioners would know that "this is the time we run our evangelization program." We do acquire an identity and self-image as we do what we do: We become evangelizers by evangelizing.

MADE, NOT BORN, NEW
PERSPECTIVES ON CHRISTIAN
INITIATION AND THE CATECHUMENATE
NOTRE DAME PRESS

BECOMING A CATHOLIC CHRISTIAN
WILLIAM H SADLIER INC

POSSIBLE OPTIONS

There are two programs of evangelization that seem to meet our first guideline for reaching out in the sense of No. 41.1 of the RCIA. One is entitled *We Care/We Share*; the other is explained in the *Parish Evangelization Planning Guide* of the Archdiocese of Atlanta. Both programs range in length from a month to six weeks, and each can be used conveniently for the evangelization phase of the yearly cycle of the RCIA.

We Care/We Share is a six-week program which invites maximum participation of parishioners in the evangelization effort. Mass mailings, door-to-door visits, and phone calls are used to invite the unchurched and the alienated to a week during which an inquirer can "taste and see" the Catholic way of life. A person can "taste" this way of life during the last week by coming to a series of liturgies and social events, or to an "open house" during which he/she can meet Catholics and learn about Catholicism. Those responding to the invitation and wanting to learn more about the Catholic way of life can attend precatechumenate "inquiry" sessions held a week or so after the completion of the *We Care/We Share* program.

We Care/We Share is well tested, having been conducted in over 35 parishes. It involves approximately 20 percent of all active parishioners in the evangelization effort. Through variations in the design this program can be used year after year as the RCIA recycles. (*We Care/We Share* is available for $3.00 from the Paulist Office for Evangelization, 3031 Fourth Street, N.E., Washington, D.C. 20017.)

The *Parish Evangelization Planning Guide* was developed by Reverend Richard A. Kieran, Secretary for Education for the Archdiocese of Atlanta. It proposes parish-based evangelization stressing the importance of small and supportive Christian communities, the formation of parish evangelizers, and the development of an annual cycle of evangelization and initiation. The evangelization program, conducted in September, includes home visitations to inactive Catholics and the unchurched, with an invitation to a week of renewal in October. The parish precatechumenate would follow this week of renewal.

The *Parish Evangelization Planning Guide* has a number of excellent ideas and suggestions concerning evangelization efforts for inactive Catholics and follow-up programs that may meet their needs. There is also a rather complete bibliography on "Evangelization within the Catholic Church" and a list of "Recommended Reading for Maturing Christians." (Copies of this planning guide can be obtained through the Paulist Office for Evangelization for $2.00.)

There is no one best way to evangelize. As a matter of fact, evangelization coordinators should plan a number of outreach efforts in order to create an understanding among both parishioners and those to whom the parish is reaching out that the community is committed to evangelization. Among other possibilities, the parish could:

- have occasional holy hours or prayer services to pray for the unchurched.
- make a consistent effort to include in the General Intercessions specific prayers for the unchurched and for the success of the parish evangelization programs.
- conduct a "Come Home for Christmas" and/or a "Come Home for Easter" evangelization program in which letters are sent out inviting the unchurched to attend the Christmas and Easter services.
- develop a series of neighborhood Bible studies to which the unchurched are invited.
- have special groups to meet the needs of the separated and divorced in the area, or other specifically alienated groups.

Coordinators for parish evangelization programs within the RCIA would do well to write the Paulist Office for Evangelization and request other information, models, and studies concerning evangelizing the unchurched. Gather as much information as you can in order to create a variety of outreach programs that are "just right" for your parish.

An important dimension that parish evangelization teams could consider is whether or not there is adequate follow-up to the outreach efforts. The *We Care/We Share* and the *Parish Evangelization* programs are excellent because they not only are effective in themselves, but conveniently fit into the parish's yearly cycle of evangelization and initiation.

Here are some other questions for parish evangelization teams to consider in developing and evaluating their programs:

1. Have all the team members read *On Evangelization in the Modern World* by Pope Paul VI? (This document is available from the Publications Office, United States Catholic Conference, 1312 Massachusetts Avenue, N.W., Washington, D.C. 20005.)
2. Have all the team members read *The Unchurched American*? (This important study, published by the Princeton Religious Research Center and the Gallup Organization in 1978, is available from the Paulist Office for Evangelization.)
3. How inviting or appealing is the parish community?
4. Is evangelization seen as God's work?
5. Are evangelization and initiation seen as both an individual and a communal responsibility?
6. Is the parish reaching out to the unchurched in deed as well as in word—in social justice activities, for example?
7. Are the evangelization efforts respectful of other Christian traditions and ecumenical relations?
8. Does the life of the parish as experienced in the liturgies, parties, and other activities communicate God's love and salvation?
9. Is the parish using modern media in the evangelization efforts?
10. Are existing groups, such as prayer groups and social action groups, utilized in outreach efforts?
11. What are evangelization programs saying to the unchurched?
12. Does the parish have a yearly cycle of evangelization and initiation?

THE PRECATECHUMENATE

This next section will describe what a developed precatechumenate program might look like in a parish. The word "precatechumenate" is used here to designate a period of time—after the evangelization efforts in the fall, and before the catechumenate.

Let's suppose that St. Raphael's parish conducted a *We Care/We Share* program in September and followed this up with a series of inquiry classes. Let's first try to understand the types of people who responded to the outreach effort, people who would be sitting in their seats at the beginning of that first class. Why did they come? What could they expect from the community of St. Raphael's?

Sitting in the first row of the large room of the parish religious education center is Merrill, who has never been baptized and has never made a firm commitment to Jesus or to living the Christian life. He talked to Andrew, a St. Raphael's parishioner, during the open house of the *We Care/We Share* program and has been wondering why Andrew seemed so happy. He came to find out.

What could the community of St. Raphael's offer Merrill? The precatechumenate for Merrill could be a time for an initial conversion to Jesus, an experience of repentance and prayer, and an experience of meeting Christians and seeing how they live, worship, and serve (No. 15). Merrill could enter the precatechumenate with the sense that this could be the first step on his journey toward the catechumenate and the other phases of the RCIA. Eventually, he could become a fully initiated member of the St. Raphael's community.

Maureen is another person attending the first class of the precatechumenate. She received a letter during the *We Care/We Share* outreach and she was curious. Maureen was baptized a Methodist, but participated only marginally in church activities until she was 17. She has not been active in any church for the past six years. Being newly married, she is interested in learning more about the Catholic Church since her husband is Catholic. She has asked her husband a number of questions about Catholicism, but he was not too sure of some of the answers himself.

What can Maureen expect from St. Raphael's? Her journey is entirely different from Merrill's in that she was baptized. Maureen would generally fit the type of person described in Chapter IV of the RCIA, that is, an uncatechized adult who is seeking to become a Catholic. It could take quite some time for the faith given to Maureen in baptism to mature (No. 296). She would need to learn about Catholic teachings, develop a personal spirituality, learn to worship as a Catholic, and continue to grow in doing works of charity and sharing the faith with others. Nos. 297–305 further explain how the community of St. Raphael's might best respond to Maureen's need to develop an adult Catholic faith. She, like Merrill, would do well to go through the precatechumenate and the rest of the stages of initiation, but always with the point of view that she is already a Christian, already a member of the baptized children of God.

Carol comes to the St. Raphael's precatechumenate class with a different situation. She has been active in Holy Redeemer Lutheran Church for most of her adult life, except for the past two years. Recently, after a long series of conversations with Vera, her Catholic neighbor, Carol has decided to inquire into Catholicism. It was Vera who suggested she come to this class.

What can Carol expect from St. Raphael's? She has a mature Christian faith and needs a different kind of pastoral care than Maureen. In order to understand the thinking of the Church on how best to care for Carol, one should read the *Rite of Reception of Baptized Christians into Full Communion with the Catholic Church* (Washington, D.C.: United States Catholic Conference, 1976). This rite is an appendix to the RCIA and gives clear guidelines as to how parishes should deal with those who are already baptized and want to become Catholics. This document points out that baptized persons like Maureen or Carol are not to be called "converts" (see the Foreword of the Appendix), nor are they to be identified in any way with the unbaptized catechumens (No. 5 of the *Rite of Reception*). It also says (No. 5) that people like Maureen and Carol will need some instruction and preparation in order to participate fully in the Catholic way of life.

Even though she is a mature Christian, Carol may decide to attend some of the precatechumenate and catechumenate classes to learn about Catholicism. More than likely, for example, she would not be familiar with the sacrament of penance. However, Carol would come to the classes with the understanding that she would share her gifts and talents developed as a Lutheran, and that her baptized status would be respected.

Through the evangelization program at St. Raphael's, Clarence also decided to come to the inquiry class. He has been separated from his wife for nine years and hasn't gone to Mass since that time. He is now interested in being reconciled with the Church and becoming a practicing Catholic once again.

What can Clarence expect? He may decide that he can benefit from attending the precatechumenate and the catechumenate classes, obtaining a sponsor from St. Raphael's, and beginning actively to participate in the life of the parish. Although he wouldn't participate in any of the initiation rites like Merrill, Maureen, or Carol, Clarence may find the initiation process offered by St. Raphael's helpful for him to "relearn" the Catholic way of life that he hasn't practiced for years. Obviously, Clarence's status as a baptized Catholic would be respected.

Those responding to evangelization and coming to the first inquiry class at St. Raphael's have a variety of needs and hopes. The Christian community of St. Raphael's will be well prepared to care pastorally for the needs of these different types of people if they are familiar with the stages of initiation for the unbaptized (Chapter I, RCIA), and are knowledgeable about preparing uncatechized adults for full reception into the Church (Chapter IV, RCIA). Those implementing the rite should also have an understanding of the *Rite of Reception of Baptized Christians into Full Communion with the Catholic Church*, and have various options available for the pastoral care of inactive Catholics.

THE PRECATECHUMENATE CLASSES

Having become acquainted with the types of people who responded to evangelization efforts at St. Raphael's, we now need to look at what their precatechumenate classes are actually like.

In addition to Merrill, Maureen, Carol, and Clarence, fourteen people attended that first Wednesday night meeting in October. The precatechumenate team was there to greet them: Fr. Stenvic, the pastor; Donna, a catechist; and Tony, a permanent deacon working in the parish adult education ministry.

The members of the team introduced themselves, as did each of the inquirers. Then Fr. Stenvic explained that the inquiry class would last for five weeks, and that an effort would be made to meet the needs of each person present. "Catholicism is a way of life," he said. "During this time we would like to give you more of an experience of what Catholicism is like. There will be a series of seminars each Wednesday night for the first four weeks, and during our class on the fifth Wednesday, we will tell you about the next step, the 'catechumenate.' We hope many of you will choose to become involved in that."

The seminars that the team from St. Raphael's used were the first four from the Life in the Spirit Seminar Series. Fr. Stenvic, Donna, and Tony had previously read the team manual entitled *The Life in the Spirit Seminars* (Notre Dame, Ind.: Charismatic Renewal Services, Inc., 1973). Knowing that the seminars have proven to be extremely successful in many parishes, they decided to adapt it for their specific needs in the precatechumenate. The four talks on God's Love, Salvation, The New Life, and Receiving God's Gift would help those attending to make an adult decision to follow Jesus. Moreover, the team manual gave Donna, Tony, and Fr. Stenvic some helpful ideas from group dynamics on how to divide the class into small groups. The manual also gave suggestions for encouraging candidates to tell their own stories and reflect on their life experience. Each person attending was given a copy of *Finding New Life in the Spirit* for his or her own meditation each day during the precatechumenate. (This pamphlet, designed for the personal use of those taking the seminars, is available from Charismatic Renewal Services, Inc., P. O. Drawer A, Notre Dame, Indiana 46556.) Any inquirer who did not have a Bible was given one.

The team decided to use part of the second Wednesday night meeting to explain the sponsor program. Each inquirer was to talk about who he/she would want as a sponsor, or whether they would want the parish to provide one. For this discussion the team found it helpful to break into small groups.

Donna, Tony, and Fr. Stenvic had decided to have a different type of prayer service each week, usually very simple. Tony led these prayer times and helped the inquirers understand how prayer is an essential part of the Catholic way of life. At the end of the third class, the inquirers were invited to the 10:00 Mass on the following Sunday. Their sponsors were to be with them during the liturgy, and the inquirers were encouraged to ask questions and discuss their feelings about the liturgy at a coffee hour afterwards. Tony had arranged for a number of the St. Raphael's parishioners to be at the social hour after Mass.

Tony always made certain that there were coffee and "goodies" available for the break during the Wednesday night classes. He felt strongly that this type of socializing was important in building a sense of community among those present. The break was a good time for people to get to know one another on a more casual basis. As the weeks went by, some attending the classes began to bring cakes and pastries themselves.

After the four-week seminar was over, Fr. Stenvic, Donna, and Tony talked about their progress during a staff meeting. They knew they were off to a good beginning. Although three people did not return after the first class, one new person, Jeremy, came during the second week, so the group seemed to be stabilizing at fifteen inquirers. Fr. Stenvic was sure that the team had enabled those in the class to experience the beginnings of the Catholic way of life. His reflection on the four weeks went something like this: "The seminars called for an adult decision for Jesus, and the small group dynamics allowed each inquirer to share his/her own journey and particular needs. In addition, each person has been matched up with a sponsor. All have attended some larger community liturgies, prayed together, and met other people from St. Raphael's; moreover they seem to be experiencing some beginnings of Christian community during our class on Wednesday nights." Tony and Donna agreed.

Donna summarized the progress of the group at the beginning of the fifth class, and then said it was time for the inquirers to make a decision. "We've been together for over a month now," she said, "and most of you seem ready to begin the next step of your journey." Donna told about this next step, the catechumenate, and how this time might meet the particular needs of those in the class. She also explained the types of journeys that each person might take. Then Donna said, "Fr. Stenvic, Tony, and I would like to have a personal interview with each of you during the coming week. Each of us will meet with those of you who were in our small groups during the seminars. We want to get to know you better and talk with you about your own goals and needs in regard to Catholicism at S. Raphael's.

We would hope to establish with each of you how you could best benefit from our time together."

The team had discussed the importance of this interview, and even did some role playing of possible interview situations. They then gave one another suggestions as to how they could make the person feel more welcome, feel less "uptight," and make sure that they were communicating with the candidate. As they were discussing the interview, Tony confided, "Sometimes I do have a tendency to 'rattle on,' without really listening deeply to what the other person is saying." The team knew that they were dealing with adults who were responsible for making choices in their lives. They wanted to make sure that the unique needs of each person—whether unbaptized, baptized, or nonpracticing Catholic—were met as much as possible.

"During the interviews we should check to find out if any candidates are involved in invalid marriages," said Fr. Stenvic. "If we begin to work on these now, perhaps some could be rectified by the time of reception into the Church at Easter." "We should also check out motivation," remarked Donna. "Sometimes people want to become Catholics, not because of a personal belief, but because their spouse is Catholic." "We should also ask about their beginning relationships with their sponsors," said Fr. Stenvic.

After the interviews, Fr. Stenvic, Donna, and Tony met and discussed each person individually. They discovered that of the four unbaptized Merrill and two others wanted to become catechumens and seemed properly motivated and prepared for this stage of their journey (see Nos. 15–16, RCIA). Larry Montgomery was one of these three. The other unbaptized person, Jeremy, just wanted to sit in on the classes for a while. Maureen and five others who were already baptized decided that they would like to participate in the catechumenate classes as a means of preparing themselves for full reception the Church during the Easter Vigil. Clarence and the two other 'icing Catholics decided to participate in the classes and ac- catechumenate as a "refresher" for them, even though articipate in any of the initiation rites. Finally, there been a faithfully practicing Lutheran until the led to attend only some of the classes of the eriodic conferences with Fr. Stenvic. She

43

felt the best way for her to become actively involved in the parish and grow in the Catholic way of life was through joining the prayer group with her Catholic friend, Vera, who was her sponsor.

The precatechumenate team at St. Raphael's was satisfied that they had done their job well. After being with these inquirers for five weeks, they were beginning to get a feel for how the catechumenate time might be shaped to give these potential new Catholics the best pastoral care. The evangelization and precatechumenate period was over. Now it was time to begin the next phase of the RCIA, the catechumenate.

Chapter Three

THE CATECHUMENATE

As we continue our journey through the RCIA, we should be aware that a parish staff or a Core Group will have worked with the rite for a number of months before coming to the catechumenate (see page 6). By this period of the rite, Core Group members and some parishioners will have developed a personal investment in the candidates. Bolstered by their previous experience in using the RCIA, the Core Group should feel confident to take up the challenge of the catechumenate.

As members of a Core Group discover how to adapt this period of the rite to the needs of their parish, they should be interested in two questions. First, what information and guidance is given in the RCIA? Second, what will the Core Group have to do to make the catechumenate a meaningful experience in the parish? These are the two questions that we will try to answer in this chapter.

THE CATECHUMENATE IN THE RCIA

Unlike evangelization and the precatechumenate, the rite of becoming catechumens and the catechumenate period are well developed within the RCIA. Nos. 14 and 68–97 explain and present the liturgical rite for celebrating the entrance of the candidates into the catechumenate. Nos. 7b, 15–20, and 98–132 are packed with suggestions for catechesis and for the celebration of liturgical rites within the catechumenate period. The problem is that after reading these sections on the catechumenate, a Core Group member may say, "I think I understand what is being said in the rite, but I'm not sure if I know what the experience is like."

The heart of the experience of being a catechumen is brought out in No. 19, sections 1–4. No. 19 in general explains that each candidate is to participate in a process of pastoral formation. Sections 1–4 describe what is to be included in this formation. The catechumen is to develop an understanding of the teachings of the Church, develop his/her spiritual life both personally and within the community, participate in liturgical rites, and learn about Christian service and sharing the Christian faith.

Let's try to get a better understanding of what is meant by pastoral formation. The experience of becoming a catechumen is not tremendously different from other experiences we have as adults. Consider someone studying for the priesthood. A seminarian is, in a sense, a "catechumen." He goes through several years of "pastoral formation" in order to learn the way of life of a priest. He is "formed" by attending theology classes, working with a spiritual director, and going to the Masses and prayer services of the seminary community. Most seminaries today stress that the seminarian get involved in some sort of apostolic work, like serving in parishes, hospitals, and jails. In this way the seminarian learns to serve by serving. There are also liturgical events during seminary formation, such as those which make him a lector or acolyte. These rites are visible expressions of the seminarian's commitment to serve God and the Church as a reader of the Word of God and as a minister at the altar. After the years of pastoral and theological formation are over, the seminarian is ordained. The period of formation is intended to prepare the seminarian for the lifestyle of an adult priestly minister in the Church.

Or again, consider the experience of people within marriage. When a man and a woman meet for the first time, they do not begin planning their marriage the day after their first date. A man and woman attracted to one another will spend time together and share their own past journeys. They will celebrate their relationship by anticipating the likes of the other or by returning to the place where they first met. They will get to know one another, perhaps discovering that each brings out special qualities in the other. They will learn to grow together. If the two develop a loving relationship, one that they would like to share and deepen throughout their lives, they may choose to marry. In a very real sense, their courtship and engagement is a "period of formation" for their lifelong adult commitment to one another in marriage.

The RCIA also talks about adults who are in the process of preparing for a life-state. The person preparing for baptism as a catechumen, or the person already baptized and wanting to become a Catholic, is forming himself/herself for a lifetime commitment as a Catholic. Such a person is like those in "formation" for marriage or the priesthood.

To talk about marriage, priesthood, and becoming a Catholic in the same breath, and in terms of the "formation" required, is even more striking when we consider that each of these adult life-states is a sacrament in the Church. The dating couple who eventually become engaged will celebrate the "formation" of their life together through the sacrament of matrimony. The seminarian will celebrate the completion of his pastoral formation through the sacrament of holy orders. Similarly, the period of pastoral formation in the catechumenate will eventually lead to the reception of baptism, confirmation, and the eucharist during the Easter Vigil.

In the thought of the RCIA, becoming a Catholic is not as easy as saying one, two, three. Becoming a Catholic—whether through baptism or through coming into full communion with the Catholic Church—could involve an extensive period of adult formation and adult decision-making. There is no precise limit set for this period of formation (No. 20), since each person makes this adult journey at his/her own pace.

The formation of these new Catholics is the responsibility of all the Catholics in the parish (No. 41). Moreover, this formation takes place progressively in the midst of the community (No. 4). What the catechumenate period will actually be like in a parish will vary because of the uniqueness of each community.

THE CATECHUMENATE IN THE PARISH

We have been discussing the principles and guidelines that the RCIA gives concerning the catechumenate. Now we shall begin to answer the second question: What might a catechumenate program look like in a parish? We shall use No. 19 as our source.

One method a Core Group can use in developing catechumenate

programs is to look at the different areas in which potential Catholics should be formed (No. 19, 1–4), and then develop programs based on these "formation requirements." What is important about No. 19 is that it is a practical description of what is involved in learning and living the Christian life. Tertullian, in the third century, said that Christians were "made, not born," and this is exactly the challenge to members of a Core Group and the parish community as they develop catechumenate programs.

Just one word of respectful hesitation, though. When we are talking about the formation of a person in the sense of No. 19, we are dealing with a marvelous mystery. How does it happen that a person who never believed in God would come to know and love him? Or that a person who had no time for the Christian community would feel attracted to it and eventually become a member? Because there is so much here beyond our understanding, we must approach the pastoral formation of people with reverence and awe. From the Christian point of view, it is God who is calling the person to be a Christian, to become a Catholic, or to become an active Catholic again. The members of the parish, Core Group, and catechetical team should never forget that they are ministers of God's love and healing presence.

As we develop what a catechumenate might look like in a parish, we shall resume our story of the RCIA at St. Raphael's. Let's see how the members of that parish went about the "formation" of those in the precatechumenate class that was ending as we closed the previous chapter. Having already met some of those in the class, we shall now meet another—Larry Montgomery. Larry is one of the nonbaptized, and is in Fr. Stenvic's small group.

Larry is 33, tall, mild-mannered, and works as an insurance salesman. He married Paula seven years ago. They have had a caring relationship and shared their lives deeply, except in matters of religion. Larry had been more interested in playing golf on Sunday morning than he was in accompanying Paula to Mass at St. Raphael's. Paula felt badly that they never talked about the meaning God had in their lives.

A year ago the relationship between Larry and Paula suddenly changed. They discovered that their three-year-old son, Eric, had leukemia. Larry couldn't face it. "Not my son," he said defiantly.

After a six-month-long struggle—hospitals, nurses, anger, hope, needles, depression, chemotherapy—Larry and Paula saw their only child die.

During Eric's illness, Fr. Stenvic came to the hospital to visit. Larry was outwardly cordial, but inwardly angry. "What can you do to save my son?" he thought. But Fr. Stenvic continued to come periodically, talking mostly with Paula.

It took a year for Larry to get over his anger and begin to accept his son's death. During this time, he and Paula became much closer to one another. "What does it all mean?" he used to ask her. "I feel so empty inside." After a while, Paula suggested that Larry stop in to see Fr. Stenvic. "What does he know!" Larry would say gruffly. But through Paula's continual support and suggestion, Larry did go and talk with Fr. Stenvic. That is how he eventually found himself in the catechumenate.

THE CATECHUMENATE "CLASSROOM"

Fr. Stenvic, Donna, and Tony continued as a catechetical team during the period of the catechumenate. Their pressing concern was how to meet the formation needs of adults, like Larry. They knew that Larry and the others would come with definite agendas. The meeting would be each Wednesday evening from 7:30 to 9:30. After a discussion, the team came up with the following approaches to meet the needs of these adults.

1. The atmosphere of the "classroom" would be informal. Luckily, the room that they had been using during the precatechumenate was almost like a living room—comfortable chairs, lamps, artwork. The team wanted to make sure that the adults coming were not treated like children or placed in a row like soldiers lining up for inspection. They wanted an atmosphere of learning, of being together, an atmosphere in which adults could feel very much at home.

2. Larry and the others attending the classes would be encouraged to make their needs known. Fr. Stenvic, Tony, and Donna assumed that Larry was self-initiating, had his own "agenda," and had certain doubts. They felt that in the end he was the person to know best whether the classes had any meaning to him. The team would encourage the candidates to ask questions and make comments.

They wanted to be sure that the material presented struck a chord in the candidate's experience. The team had also decided to ask Larry and one other candidate to meet with them as team members after the beginning of the catechumenate. This would be a way to insure that the team and the class were not traveling down two different roads. As Donna said during the meeting, "These adults are responsible and accountable at home and on the job; we should treat them the same way when they are here."

3. The team decided to continue small group meetings during part of the class time, with each team member leading one of the groups. Tony was enthused about this. "Being in small groups," he said, "allows each person to be known as a unique human being with feelings, doubts, joys, and periods of confusion. The small groups we have been having allow our candidates to participate, tell their own experiences, and develop relationships."

Fr. Stenvic, Tony, and Donna had already experienced themselves to be a small Christian community as they worked together. They hoped that members of their small groups would have this same experience of community over the months that they would spend together in the "classes." The whole class would learn to experience themselves as a Christian community, but many of the relationships that would make this larger community memorable would come from getting to know the others in the small groups. Fr. Stenvic knew that Larry had experienced some definite changes in his life through his primary relationship with Paula. Perhaps he could experience growth in the Christian life through relationships with others in the Wednesday night classes.

4. The final approach that the team discussed concerned the fact that they should model what they were trying to teach. They decided to come together and pray before the Wednesday night meetings and spend time together in preparation for the classes. The team members were aware that they were God's and St. Raphael's ministers for the pastoral formation of those involved in the catechumenate classes.

The team met together on another night to discuss the general areas that should be covered in the classes. They spent time talking about No. 19, sections 1–4, and decided to cover as many of the areas mentioned in these sections as possible. They also wanted to stress that the Christian life was not just something that the candidates would "learn about," but rather experience as a style of life.

Listed below are some topical areas that Donna, Tony, and Fr. Stenvic came up with that would be meaningful for the formation of the candidates during the Wednesday night classes. These topics are in no special order.

- the meaning of the sacraments, especially baptism, confirmation, and the eucharist
- God's plan of salvation history
- explanation of the liturgical year
- the Catholic commitment to social justice
- the need for evangelization and sharing the Christian faith
- Catholic sexual morality—abortion, birth control, and divorce
- the meaning of the liturgical rites of the Church
- Catholic teaching on God the Father, Jesus, and the Holy Spirit
- faith journeys of the saints in the Catholic tradition, for example, Paul and Augustine
- the meaning of conversion in one's life, on moral, intellectual, and spiritual levels
- the importance of Sacred Scripture, and praying the Scriptures in one's daily life
- ways of praying, and the meaning of prayer in the Christian life
- spiritual direction and interpreting the actions of the Holy Spirit in one's life
- what it means to live by faith
- the importance of participating in the liturgies of the Church
- the Christian as one who serves and carries on the work of Christ
- the corporal and spiritual works of mercy
- the meaning of relationships with sponsors
- the Church and ecumenical relations
- living in a Christian community

51

The team was satisfied with these general topical areas, but they knew that they wanted more during the two-hour class times than a presentation on a topic. The team decided that, as much as possible, the candidates should "experience" what was being presented. As they discussed the need for experiential learning, Tony wrote down the following list of exercises and activities that would enable the candidates to be formed in the Christian life by experiencing it. The candidates could:

- experience and discuss the rite of becoming catechumens and the other liturgical rites during their Wednesday night class.
- go to weddings, infant baptisms, communal celebrations of the sacrament of reconciliation, and other activities in the life of the parish. The candidates could talk about these experiences with their sponsors or in the small groups on Wednesday nights.
- take a tour of St. Raphael's Church to look at the vestments, liturgical books, and other items that the candidates see during the liturgies.
- learn how to "pray" and meditate on the Scriptures read at Mass each Sunday, and have an actual experience of praying these Sunday readings during class.
- learn how to plan a prayer service and then experience what they planned.
- experience the minor exorcisms (RCIA, Nos. 109–118) and the blessing of catechumens (Nos. 119–124) toward the end of a class period.
- learn to "pray" the Scriptures and experience this in class.
- be taught about the different kinds of prayer books available, such as *Night Prayer*, from the Liturgy of the Hours (available from the Publications Office, United States Catholic Conference, 1312 Massachusetts Avenue, N.W., Washington, D.C. 20005), or *Christian Prayer* (New York: The Catholic Book Publishing Co., 1976), and experience, for example, a service from *Night Prayer*.
- plan and participate in a paraliturgical penance service, either before or after the presentation was given on the sacrament of penance.

- be taught the importance of keeping a journal throughout the time of formation and be given experiences of different types of journal keeping.
- in conjunction with the presentation on social justice, take a field trip to a social action center.

The team knew that there were more things the candidates could do in order to experience the Christian life, but they felt that the list above gave them a good start.

Donna, Tony, and Fr. Stenvic were getting excited at this point in their meeting. They were almost ready to begin designing the content and activities for each class of the catechumenate. However, Fr. Stenvic said that they should also begin to form a lending library that all the candidates could use. Here are some of the items that the team wanted to include in their library:

Christ Among Us by Anthony Wilhelm (New York: Paulist Press, 1975)

The Faith of Catholics by Richard Chilson (New York: Paulist Press, 1975)

The Jesus People by John J. Ryan (Chicago: Life in Christ, 1970)

A New Catechism (New York: Herder and Herder, 1969)

Christian and Catholic magazines

Christian books on the spiritual masters, morality, spirituality, Scripture, and other topics of interest

Cassette tapes on prayer, community living, liturgical topics, and other areas of interest

At this point—and it was the third time that the team had met together to plan for the catechumenate—they decided to begin outlining the content and activities for each catechumenate class. Generally, the three wanted to fill the two-hour Wednesday night classes with presentations, small and large group discussions, and exercises in which experience was stressed and the candidates would learn by "doing." Sometimes there would be presentations, role playing, or discussions on short articles or selections from books. Of course, the coffee break was always held sacred, being considered essential in forming the life of their Wednesday night community. Regardless of how Fr. Stenvic and the team presented the Christian way of life, they knew that the candidates would have to do a lot of reflecting on

53

their own experience. This would be the only way for them to discover how the gospel message had meaning in their lives.

When the team came to a consensus about a schedule that would meet the needs of these candidates, Tony printed up the schedule of presentations and activities for each class and gave a copy to the candidates. He also gave copies to the sponsors and Core Group members, and arranged to have this schedule posted in the vestibule of the Church in order to encourage interested parishioners to attend.

Larry found these Wednesday night classes to be challenging and meaningful. He was discovering that being a Christian is not some "pie in the sky" activity, but a way of life that touched every part of his life—as he was living it.

THE CANDIDATES MEET THE COMMUNITY

As the Core Group from St. Raphael's was meeting before the start of the catechumenate, they were aware that there were other ways that the candidates could be formed in the Christian way of life in addition to the experience of the classroom. The group specifically discussed No. 19.2, which talks about how a candidate can learn the Christian way of life through the help and example of sponsors and other members of the parish community. It was at this point that the group discussed the possibilities of a "Community Hour" at St. Raphael's during the catechumenate period.

Helen, the Core Group member responsible for bringing together the candidates and members of the community, spoke up. "We have talked about how the sponsors could relate to the candidates, but we haven't solved the problem of how others in the parish could get to know them, and vice versa. Although I haven't worked out all the details, I think that one solution would be to have a 'Community Hour' on Sunday mornings during the catechumenate. The purpose would be for the parishioners to meet and get to know the candidates."

Helen continued, "Here's how the program could work. Each Sunday morning, immediately after the 10:00 Mass—the one that the candidates and their sponsors attend—the candidates and their sponsors could come to our social hall and meet with active Catholics. I could see us inviting active Catholics or other Christians involved in these activities, organizations, or movements. Let me read you my list." Here is Helen's list:

- Cursillo
- religious education at St. Raphael's
- Marriage Encounter
- diocesan agencies
- young adult retreat centers
- the parish social action committee
- the Divorced and Separated Catholics group
- Birthright
- the Catholic Worker movement
- the charismatic renewal prayer group
- the Legion of Mary
- the parish council
- the teen club
- the choir

After some discussion, the Core Group came up with other possibilities. The candidates could meet the lay ministers of the eucharist, liturgy committee members, parish evangelizers, newly initiated Catholics from previous years, ushers, permanent deacons, representatives of religious orders, Core Group members, and active Christians from other denominations in the area. Donna also commented that any person could be invited to share his/her Christian journey. An older person, or one who had suffered a lot, could tell the candidates what meaning Jesus had in his/her life.

Helen said, "The 'Community Hour' could begin with coffee and an informal social gathering after the Mass. Then I would introduce whomever we have invited for that Sunday—members of the parish council, for example. After all the persons attending had introduced themselves, the parish council president could speak about the work of the council and tell about what being a Catholic and serving on the council means to her. Other parish council members could tell their 'story' as well. Depending on the number attending, later conversation could occur in the large group, or small groups could be formed. It's important that those presenting get to know the candidates."

Fr. Stenvic broke in at this point and commented, "One of the best features of these Sunday morning periods would be the feeling among some of the candidates that they were truly welcomed by our community. It might be a good idea too, Helen, if you had a short period of prayer either at the beginning or at the end of the hour."

Then Helen told the Core Group of another idea that came to light as she and Donna were talking earlier. "We decided to coordinate the activities of the 'Community Hour' and the catechumenate classes whenever we can. For example, Donna told me that there would be one class on the topic of social justice, and I said that we could arrange to get some representatives from the Catholic Worker movement to speak the following Sunday. Hearing these people speak should make the issue of social justice come alive for the candidates."

The Core Group liked what Helen was presenting, but they had some suggestions. Other members of the parish, especially those new to the area, should be invited, as should the spouses and families of the candidates. Evelyn, the liturgy coordinator, then said, "I think that another advantage of the 'Community Hour' is that it gives the candidates an idea of the different types of Christian service that they might get involved in, either now or at some later time. Maybe some would want to be in the choir, or on the social justice committee. You might suggest to those presenting, Helen, that they invite the candidates to their meetings or activities."

At the close of their discussion of the Sunday "Community Hour" as well as other areas related to No. 19.2, the Core Group was satisfied that they had carried out their responsibility of pastoral formation in this area. They had at least done what they felt they could do this year.

LITURGICAL CELEBRATIONS

As they continued to prepare for the pastoral formation of the candidates, the Core Group gave Evelyn and her team the primary responsibility for planning the rite of becoming catechumens and the other liturgical rites of the catechumenate. Evelyn especially wanted to stress the importance of the rite of becoming catechumens (No. 14). This rite celebrates publicly the inquirer's decision to become a Christian and the Church's welcoming the inquirer into the community. Through this rite, each nonbaptized inquirer becomes known as a catechumen.

The liturgy team met on two occasions. After reading the rite of becoming catechumens and the rites of the catechumenate given in the RCIA, they discussed how these liturgical celebrations could best give Larry and the other candidates real experiences of God's presence among them. The team wanted to involve the community as much as possible, not only because the initiation was to take place in the midst of the community (No. 4), but because some members of the parish would want to be there. As Evelyn said at their first meeting, "I think it would be thrilling for a person on the evangelization team to see someone initiated through liturgical rites, especially when that person played a big part in the candidate's coming to St. Raphael's a few months earlier."

One of the items that Evelyn and the team discussed at their first meeting was whether or not the catechumens should be dismissed after the liturgy of the word (No. 19.3). "The RCIA does recommend dismissing them," commented Evelyn, "but allows catechumens to remain through the Mass because of pastoral reasons." After some discussion the team felt they needed other opinions, so they decided to present this issue at the next Core Group meeting. In the end, the liturgy team did decide that the catechumens should remain. Here are some of their reasons. Larry was already somewhat familiar with the Mass because he had gone with Paula, especially during the past year. Other catechumens had some experience with the Mass as well. Moreover, those who were in the catechumenate class, and already baptized, really should be encouraged to worship with their fellow Christians, even though their participation is limited according to the norms of the Directory on Ecumenism (1967) and No. 301 of the RCIA. Another factor was the positive value of having the community which was learning together during the Wednesday night classes worship together on Sunday mornings. This would include the nonbaptized candidates, those seeking full communion with the Church, as well as the previously inactive Catholics. It was a result of this discussion that the team decided to have the 10:00 Mass on Sunday as the time for all the candidates and their sponsors to come. This Mass also made it convenient for most to attend the Community Hour afterward.

On their second evening of being together and familiarizing themselves with the rites, the liturgical team made some other decisions. First of all, they wanted two of the candidates to work with them on their team to insure that the rites would be celebrations of the entire community. They also decided to use different rites throughout the catechumenate period. After consulting the parish calendar and deciding to have the rite of becoming catechumens in November, the team kept in mind their various options for liturgical rites mentioned in Nos. 98–105 of the RCIA.

The issue of pastoral care for those candidates who were already baptized came up during the second meeting. "The people like Maureen and Carol are not to participate in the same liturgical rites as the catechumens," said Evelyn, "yet we do want to make them feel welcome and feel that they are becoming a part of our community." Fr. Stenvic pointed out that special recognition was in order for those already baptized but seeking full communion with the Church. The priest felt that this recognition was in line with No. 300 of the RCIA and with the spirit of the *Rite of Reception of Baptized Christians into Full Communion with the Catholic Church.*

After listening to Fr. Stenvic, the team decided to include those already baptized in each liturgical rite. For example, their names would be mentioned during the General Intercessions, or they would be introduced to the parishioners after communion on the Sunday that the rite of becoming catechumens was celebrated. As the liturgical team prepared for each of the rites during the catechumenate, they always asked themselves how the baptized candidates could participate, and then adapted the rites accordingly.

Throughout the catechumenate, Evelyn and her team were continually challenged to make the rites "speak" to the experience of the candidates and the community. When preparing for the rite of becoming catechumens, for example, the team talked extensively about where the candidates and their sponsors would stand at the beginning of the rite (No. 73), so that the candidates might feel that they were being welcomed into a Christian community. Another example of trying to make the rites meaningful came up when the team was preparing for the rite of blessing for the catechumens (Nos. 119–124). Evelyn said, "If we are going to have this rite in the classrooms on Wednesday night, how are we going to involve the candidates who are already baptized?" The team proposed this solution: All baptized persons present would lay hands on the catechumens while the community prayed for them. In their preparation for the various rites, the team discovered that each rite demanded thought and planning so as to make it a meaningful community celebration.

For Evelyn and her team, a satisfying aspect of celebrating the rites was the fact that each rite was a "teachable moment" for the candidates, the sponsors, and the entire community. The experience of celebrating the rite of becoming catechumens allowed for a threefold benefit: (1) an explanation and a "talking through" the rite during the Wednesday night class; (2) actually experiencing the rite at the 10:00 Mass on Sunday; and (3) reflecting on that experience in the small groups during the next Wednesday night class. Sponsors told Evelyn that some of the rites were very prayerful experiences for them. But one comment that Evelyn will find hard to forget came from Mrs. Jacobson, a longtime parishioner at St. Raphael's. After the rite of becoming catechumens, she said to Evelyn, "Being here today has made me feel proud to be a part of St. Raphael's parish."

Through the classes, the Sunday Community Hour, the sponsors, and the liturgical celebrations, the Core Group at St. Raphael's knew that they had provided many opportunities for the "pastoral formation" of the candidates. They felt that they had met the challenge of Christian formation in No. 19, 1–4. Interviews with the candidates would help them see to what extent this "formation" was actually taking place. The Core Group gave the catechetical team the primary responsibility for the interviews.

THE INTERVIEWS

Fr. Stenvic, Donna, and Tony had been working with the candidates from October through March. Almost a half year had passed since some of them had responded to the *We Care/We Share* evangelization appeal. Although they had talked with all the candidates and were developing deeper relationships in their small groups, the three team members now wanted to have a more formal interview with the catechumens because the rite of election was approaching.

This rite of election, held on the First Sunday of Lent, is the turning point of the catechumenate (No. 23). It celebrates the candidate's intention to receive baptism, confirmation, and the eucharist at the Easter Vigil, and recognizes the community's decision that the candidates are adequately prepared to take this step (No. 133). After celebrating this rite, the catechumens are called the "elect."

The team knew that this interview with the catechumens should be given some thought and preparation. "How can we really find out if the catechumens are ready to go forward in their initiation process and become the 'elect'?" asked Donna. "Maybe some might choose to remain in the catechumenate for a longer period of time." After considering the possibilities, Donna decided to design an interview form that reflected the goals of the pastoral formation/catechumenate program at St. Raphael's. Since the Core Group had based their planning on No. 19, 1–4, and the catechetical team used this same section to govern the design and content of their classes, Donna came up with the idea of reflecting these "formation criteria" in the actual interview form. She asked Tony and Fr. Stenvic to help her and the three of them prepared an interview sheet entitled "A Pause along the Journey." Here is what it looked like. (See page 65.)

Tony noted that this interview form asked most of the questions that they were interested in discussing with the catechumens. He also told Donna and Fr. Stenvic that, in his opinion, the interviews should not involve slavishly going down each question, like doing a tax form. Rather the interview should be a time when each catechumen could talk about his/her thoughts and feelings up to this point of the journey. "These interviews are a real opportunity for our continuing to develop a pastoral relationship with each of the candidates," said Tony. Donna and Fr. Stenvic nodded in agreement. The catechumens received a copy of the "Pause along the Journey" about a week before their interview. Donna also gave a copy of the interview form to the sponsors and to the members of the Core Group.

The team decided to have a more formal interview with the catechumens about three weeks before the First Sunday of Lent. At this same time, they had less formal interviews with the baptized non-Catholics and the nonpracticing Catholics. Their persisting goal was to have a personal talk with each candidate every four to six weeks during the time of the catechumenate classes. Sometimes these talks would center around particular topics, like abortion or birth control, or sometimes the candidates would want to talk about other personal areas. In addition to these talks or interviews, more items on the candidate's personal agenda came to light when the small groups met. This was especially true once an atmosphere of trust and confidence was established. With the pastoral care given in the personal interviews and through the more personal discussions in the small groups, the team felt that they were attending to the unique formation needs of each person coming to St. Raphael's.

When it was time for the interview with the catechumens, Fr. Stenvic was looking forward to talking with Larry Montgomery. The two had known each other since Fr. Stenvic visited Larry and Paula when Eric was sick. Their interview took place in the priest's office about three weeks before the First Sunday of Lent.

Larry entered rather hurriedly. As he came in, Fr. Stenvic got up from his desk, greeted him, and sat down in a chair near Larry. "It's good to see you again," Fr. Stenvic began. Larry nodded, was silent for a moment, and then said, "I'm glad we could talk today, Fr. Stenvic. When you asked me to take home the 'Pause along the Journey' form a week ago, I was sort of afraid. Sometimes it's hard to get in touch with what has been going on inside."

"It sounds like we have something to talk about today, Larry," said Fr. Stenvic. "I like what you're saying about listening to what is going on inside. I know that you have felt very hurt and angry in the past, especially after Eric's death."

"I guess you knew that I didn't care much for you or anyone else from St. Raphael's at that time," replied Larry. "I was so angry at God, at you . . . I don't know. It was all so confusing."

"Have those feelings changed at all, especially since you have been in the catechumenate?" asked Fr. Stenvic.

"Somewhat," said Larry rather hesitantly. "I don't know quite how to put it, but I feel more hopeful now."

"Hopeful?" repeated Fr. Stenvic.

"Well, maybe what I am really trying to say is that I feel loved. Paula and I have grown much closer since Eric's death. She has been so good in supporting me while I have been coming on Wednesday nights and Sundays. Richard and Liz Armstrong, my sponsors, have invited Paula and me over for dinner, and have gone to Mass with us. I can vividly recall a conversation with Richard when I felt like quitting; he helped me decide to continue. Even when I come on Wednesday night, I enjoy seeing Clarence, Maureen, and Donna. They accept me and love me. I have never experienced anything like it before."

Fr. Stenvic was silent for a while, and then said, "Maybe what you are experiencing, Larry, is God's love for you."

Larry looked at Fr. Stenvic and said, "I have been thinking about that myself. Paula and I have begun to read the Bible every day. When I read the Scriptures, and Paula and I talk about what they mean to us, I can't help but feel that God does love me. I guess what I am experiencing is something that I have been looking for, but never knew where to find it. I had an empty spot, a hollow space inside that could not be filled. It was like eating and eating, but still feeling hungry. But after experiencing these last six months, actually this past year and a half, with Paula, you, the Armstrongs, Maureen—I feel like some of that hollow space is filling up. I guess that is why I said I feel hopeful."

Fr. Stenvic was listening intently. "Tell me more about this feeling of hope, Larry."

"I guess it's associated with a new sense that I feel about myself, a new identity. I am beginning to feel a part of this community. Don't get me wrong, it's not like I want to wear a big sign that says, 'I like it here at St. Raphael's,' but I do look forward to coming to Mass each Sunday with Paula, meeting the Armstrongs, and then going to the 'Community Hour' after Mass. I do find that meaningful."

Fr. Stenvic had a gleam in his eye and said, "Yes, I have enjoyed those Community Hours myself. But, go on."

"Well," said Larry, "Paula and I have been reexamining areas of our life and have made some changes. We have been reading the Scripture lessons for the Mass of the day. Scripture is filled with hope, and that is one of the things I need to hear. I also have been reading chapters from *Christ among Us*, mostly trying to fill in some of the areas that I have become curious about."

The priest then reflected aloud, "It seems to me, Larry, that the catechumenate has been very good for you." "It hasn't been all roses," Larry replied, "but I do feel good about being where I am, about being a Christian." The two talked for about a half hour more. Then Larry said, "I do feel hopeful, yet I know that I still have a way to go before I feel fully a part of the Catholic way of life at St. Raphael's.

"I hear what you are saying," said Fr. Stenvic. "Perhaps you might choose to get more involved in the parish. You have been active on our team with Donna, Tony, and myself. But now you may be in a good position to give to others, just as others have given their love to you. And there is another thing to consider. You probably won't feel fully a part of our community until you are baptized and become a member of the Catholic Church at the Easter Vigil."

"I will think about that some more," said Larry as he nodded his head affirmatively.

"Well, Larry, we have been talking for quite a while. But let me ask you directly. Do you feel you are ready to become one of the 'elect' on the first Sunday of Lent?"

"Yes, I do," replied Larry, "and I would like the Armstrongs to be my godparents. I have talked this over with Paula, and we feel it is right. I want to become a Catholic at St. Raphael's."

With a smile on his face, Fr. Stenvic stated, "I feel you are right in your decision. I have appreciated your presence and participation in our classes. You have some real gifts and talents, Larry. I will look forward to seeing you again."

"Thanks for the time to talk," said Larry as he shook hands with Fr. Stenvic. "I'll see you on Sunday."

After all the interviews, Fr. Stenvic, Tony, and Donna met and discussed each person. There were three catechumens who were ready to become the "elect" on the First Sunday of Lent: Larry, Merrill, and one other. One catechumen chose to wait and consider the decision again next year. The others in the class, including Maureen and Carol, were still walking along their journey to full reception into the Catholic Church. Clarence and the other previously nonpracticing Catholics were becoming more active again, and no one had dropped out.

Donna reported on the progress at the Core Group meeting.

The members of this group commented that, for the most part, their catechumenate programs had been successful in the formation of the candidates. They then began to discuss their specific plans for the next phases of the RCIA at St. Raphael's—the period of illumination and the sacraments of initiation.

ST. RAPHAEL'S PARISH
A PAUSE ALONG THE JOURNEY

Since October we have walked along the path to full initiation into the Catholic Church at St. Raphael's parish. We want to pause now and reflect on our journey up to this point. The following questions should be helpful.

1. Do you feel that you are experiencing a conversion to Christ and to a new way of life in the Catholic Church?

2. Do you have an understanding of God's love for you and of his loving plan of salvation in which you share? Are you beginning to see how this love is expressed through your participation in the Catholic community of St. Raphael's parish?

3. Do you feel concerned or puzzled about any teachings of the Catholic Church?

4. The Catholic faith is a way of life, a new way of living. Do you feel that you have a growing desire to:
   a. pray and read Scripture?
   b. live your faith such that you expect to experience God's love for you, and allow the Holy Spirit to lead you in living the Catholic faith?
   c. exercise charity toward your neighbor, even to the point of self-renunciation?
   d. live according to Catholic moral teachings?

5. Do you feel a growing yearning to spread the gospel and become involved in various areas of service within the Church?

6. Do you have any questions about your participation in the Mass, or in other liturgical rites of the Catholic Church?

7. Do you have a supportive relationship with your sponsor?

8. Do you want another person and/or family, other than your present sponsor, to be your godparent at baptism?

9. Do you feel a new identity developing within yourself, an identity as a Catholic?

10. Do you wish to become one of the "elect" on the first Sunday of Lent, and be fully initiated into the Catholic Church through baptism, confirmation, and receiving the eucharist during the Easter Vigil?

Note: You may wish to discuss these questions with your sponsor. We on the pastoral team may also be talking with your sponsors to seek their opinion on how you are progressing along your journey.

Chapter Four

ELECTION AND THE SACRAMENTS OF INITIATION

Let's pause a moment and look at where we are on our initiation journey. Here is the roadmap of the RCIA that we consulted before:

evangelization and precatechumenate	period 1
rite of becoming catechumens	stage 1
catechumenate	period 2
rite of election (First Sunday of Lent)	**stage 2**
illumination (during Lent)	**period 3 We are here**
sacraments of initiation (Easter Vigil)	**stage 3**
postbaptismal catechesis (Easter-Pentecost)	period 4

The boldface type highlights the stages and the period we are discussing in this chapter.

We are at a very important juncture in our journey. The rite of election is the turning point of the whole catechumenate (No. 23). The period of Lent, a period of illumination or purification and enlightenment, completes the spiritual and catechetical formation of the candidates (No. 153). Receiving the eucharist as part of the sacraments of initiation at the Easter Vigil is the culmination of the entire initiation process (No. 36).

A Core Group arriving at the present juncture may wish to pause and pray in order to plan for the period of Lent and the sacraments of initiation. The group will want to consider two questions.

First, what are the guidelines and suggestions of the RCIA for the period of illumination and the sacraments of initiation? Second, how could the parish go about implementing this part of the rite?

LENT AND THE EASTER VIGIL
ACCORDING TO THE RCIA

Of all the periods and stages of initiation, the RCIA gives the most complete guidelines for the rite of election, the period of illumination, and the sacraments of initiation. Any Core Group would do well to read—savor, meditate on, pray about—these sections of the RCIA before deciding on activities for the parish.

There are a few especially important guidelines. Traditionally, Lent has been approached as a time when members of a parish community prepare themselves for Easter. Some parishes have prayer services or say the stations of the cross. In accord with this tradition, the RCIA (No. 21) speaks of Lent as a time when both the community and the elect prepare for Easter. Both are to do penance; both are to prepare either for their baptism or for the renewal of baptismal promises. Lent is a time for individual and communal conversion.

The period of illumination during Lent is different from the catechumenate. This is a period of spiritual recollection for the candidates (No. 25), which is accomplished mostly through the rites of the scrutinies and the presentations of the creed and the Lord's Prayer. The scrutinies (Nos. 154–180) are liturgical rites which help to purify and intensify the conversion of the elect. The presentations (Nos. 181–192) give the candidates the experience of publicly receiving the tradition of faith and prayer of the Church. Lent is like a retreat for those preparing for baptism or full reception into the Catholic Church. The members of the parish community are asked to be with the candidates during this time, especially at the rite of election, the scrutinies, the presentations, and the Easter Vigil (No. 41, 3–4). The presence of the faithful gives the candidates the sense that they are becoming a part of a supportive community. And the faithful themselves benefit from participating in these rites.

As the Core Group is planning for the rite of election, the period of Lent, and the sacraments of initiation, group members will want to keep both the candidates and the entire community in mind. Nos. 51–55 suggest the "prime times" for having the appropriate liturgies. The rite of election should be on the First Sunday of Lent, the first scrutiny on the Third Sunday of Lent, the preparatory rites on Holy Saturday, with the final initiation taking place during the Easter Vigil. The preparatory rites (Nos. 193–207) on Holy Saturday involve a time of recollection and prayer with the celebration of such rites as the recitation of the profession of faith or the rite of opening the ears and mouth.

Becoming a Christian involves plunging into the death of Jesus and rising with him to new life; that is why the Easter Vigil is the climax to the entire initiation process (No. 8). The activities of this period, such as the scrutinies and preparatory rites, make sense only if they are seen as leading up to full participation in the death and resurrection of Jesus through being baptized, confirmed, and receiving the eucharist during the Easter Vigil.

A Core Group will need to trust that the various rites will indeed be prayerful and "conversion" experiences for the candidates and the community. These liturgies are the People of God at prayer, a people carrying within themselves an incredibly rich tradition. Helping the candidates and the community "experience" themselves at prayer, and then reflect on this experience, can be a memorable gift from the Core Group to the community. This period of time requires a lot of work and preparation; it is the most intense time of the initiation journey. The Core Group, as well as members of the community and the candidates, could with benefit fast and pray during Lent. They could pray especially that God would bring about an intense conversion of the candidates and a deeper conversion of the baptized.

LENT AND THE EASTER VIGIL IN THE PARISH

We have been reflecting on the rites and the period of illumination in the "abstract," as generally set forth in the guidelines of the RCIA. We shall now try to make the abstract "concrete" and see what the period of Lent and the sacraments of initiation are like at St. Raphael's parish.

THE LENTEN "CLASSROOM"

Let's join Donna, Tony, Fr. Stenvic, Larry, and the other candidate as they meet to plan activities for their Lenten classroom on Wednesday nights. It is almost a month before Ash Wednesday. The five know that basically they have three tasks: to prepare for the rite of election which is to be held on the First Sunday of Lent; to design "classes" for the Wednesday evenings during the Lenten period; and to prepare for the sacraments of initiation celebrated during the Easter Vigil.

In Tony's opinion, the first task of preparing for the rite of election could be taken care of rather easily. "I think we should discuss the rite during our Wednesday night class, a week and a half before the First Sunday of Lent. We could then insure that the candidates understand the meaning of the rite. If we are going to have special prayers at this liturgy for those candidates already baptized, we need to go over that part with them as well. We should discuss the rite on Wednesday night, and then have a practice with the candidates, sponsors, and godparents on the following Sunday. With this preparation everyone concerned should feel comfortable enough when the bishop comes to celebrate the rite of election."

"Sounds good to me," said Donna.

"What I am concerned about, though," mused Fr. Stenvic, "is how we can make our Lenten classroom truly a prayerful and spiritual experience for the candidates."

"There is one paragraph in the RCIA that gives me a definite clue," commented Donna. "No. 25 talks about Lent as a time of spiritual recollection which is accomplished mostly through the scrutinies, presentations, and other rites. I think we should 'teach' from these rites. After all, it is the content of these liturgies that gives the meaning of Lent."

"What do you mean?" questioned Larry.

"Take the third scrutiny as an example," replied Donna. "It teaches that Jesus is the source of new life for all of us, just as he was the source of new life in raising Lazarus from the dead."

"I think I understand," said Larry. "What you would try to do in our classroom is to help us understand, experience, and reflect on

70

the meaning of these rites . . . this would be different from the cate-chumenate."

"I agree with what both of you are saying," interrupted Fr. Stenvic. "I would also like to see us continue the other activities we have in our 'catechumenate classroom,' you know, the small groups, the coffee breaks, and the activities for learning about the Christian life by experiencing it."

"All those activities are very important to me," said Larry, agreeing with Fr. Stenvic. "I would like to see them continue also."

After the five talked a while longer, Donna asked Tony if he would make a list of each of the Wednesdays and then write what activities would occur each week. Here is what he wrote:

Wednesday before the rite of election
- teaching on the season of Lent
- general review of the catechumenate
- small groups, which would include discussion of the Ash Wednesday service for those who attended

Wednesday of the first week of Lent
- teaching on the first scrutiny
- practice for the first scrutiny
- small groups
- review the different ways of praying that were taught during the catechumenate

Wednesday of the second week of Lent
- teaching on the second scrutiny
- small groups
- teaching on the rite of penance
- experience a paraliturgical penance service
- practice for the presentation of the creed

Wednesday of the third week of Lent
- presentation of the creed service, with sponsors and members from the St. Raphael's community invited

Wednesday of the fourth week of Lent
- teaching on the third scrutiny
- small groups
- practice for the presentation of the Lord's Prayer
- general explanation of the sacraments of initiation, with each candidate receiving a copy of these liturgies

Wednesday of the fifth week of Lent
- presentation of the Lord's Prayer, with sponsors and the members from the St. Raphael's community invited

Wednesday before the Easter Vigil
- teaching on the sacraments of initiation
- discussion of preparatory rites to be held the following Saturday afternoon
- discussion of the Easter Vigil rites and Scripture readings
- large group reflection on the period of illumination

After Tony listened to the team's suggestions and finished writing down the activities for each Wednesday evening, there were still some questions remaining.

Larry spoke up, "Why the stress on the sacrament of penance during the class time?"

"That's a very important part of Lent, Larry," said Fr. Stenvic. "The *Rite of Reception of Baptized Christians into Full Communion with the Catholic Church* (No. 9) states that those coming into the Church should confess their sins beforehand. Protestants generally have not experienced the Catholic rite of penance, and the rest of you in the class are not familiar with it either. This is why we not only want to tell you about it in class, but let all of you experience a type of communal penance service. After your baptism, you will want to make use of the sacrament of penance yourself."

Tony mentioned that he would announce later on that all the candidates were invited to attend the communal celebrations of the sacrament of penance that St. Raphael's parish would be having during Lent. "This would be a good way for all of you to experience the fact that many parishioners are preparing for Easter, just as you are," said Tony.

"I understand," replied Larry. "I also feel comfortable with the types of activities that we have planned, such as the teachings, small groups, and the different experiences with the liturgies. What we've planned seems to meet my needs, and I think it would meet the needs of the other candidates."

"I have one comment, though," replied Donna. "We should ask our coordinator of publicity to inform the sponsors and parishioners that they are invited to the presentations of the creed and the Lord's Prayer. I think that these could be meaningful evenings for anyone who would want to come. I have read these liturgies and feel that even I would benefit from attending. I have been saying the Our Father and the creed for years, and sometimes take their meaning for granted."

After the team finished their meeting, they prayed that God would bless their efforts. Their hope was that their "Lenten classroom" would truly be an occasion for meaningful prayer and conversion among each of the candidates and the staff, as well as among the sponsors and members of the parish who would attend the presentations.

REND YOUR HEARTS

When the Core Group from St. Raphael's met during January for a planning meeting, there were two new people in attendance: Henry and Phyllis Johnson. Helen, the coordinator of the Community Hour, had brought the Johnsons to the meeting for a special reason. When it came time for "new business," Helen spoke up and said she would like to get the opinion of the Core Group about what to do for Lent.

"What do you have up your sleeve this time?" questioned Donna, remembering the enthusiastic presentation that Helen gave on the Sunday Community Hour a few months earlier.

"I have been reading the RCIA and have been doing some thinking," Helen began. "We are having a very good experience with the Community Hour during the catechumenate, but the period of Lent seems to call for something different. Lent is a time of spiritual recollection, for both the candidates and the community. What we need for Lent at St. Raphael's is a program that will involve the whole parish and the candidates in making this a special time of individual and communal preparation for Easter."

"The theory sounds good," Donna reflected, "but I am not aware of any such programs."

"I did some investigating," responded Helen, "and the Lenten program I feel would best meet our needs is called *Rend Your Hearts*. It was developed by the Office of Social Development of the Archdiocese of Washington, D.C. (2800 Otis St., N.E., Washington, D.C. 20018). There are other commendable and successful programs available, but certain features of *Rend Your Hearts* attract me. This program centers around the Sunday readings for each of the weeks of Lent. Small groups from the parish are formed and meet each week for about an hour and a half. The group members discuss the readings, share their faith, commit themselves to individual or group actions, and end the meeting with a short prayer service. I'll pass out a sample for the Fourth Sunday of Lent so you can see what I am talking about." (See pages 85-87.)

After the Core Group members read the handout, Helen continued. "We could publicize the *Rend Your Hearts* program, train small group leaders, and then have as many small groups as we need to take care of the number of people responding. We could distribute the *Rend Your Hearts* forms at all the Masses on the Sunday before the week the groups meet. That way, individuals, families, or organizations could participate in *Rend Your Hearts* even if they choose not to join one of the groups."

"It sounds like a tremendous idea, Helen," commented Fr. Stenvic, "but it would take quite a bit of work."

"Luckily," responded Helen, "Henry and Phyllis Johnson have volunteered to coordinate this program at St. Raphael's. I have discussed most of the details with them, and, pending the judgment of the group, I think it would be a good idea to try it in our parish this year."

Then Henry Johnson spoke up. "I am personally committed to *Rend Your Hearts*. Phyllis and I experienced a similar program last year in our old parish, and it was very successful. The people in the groups meet on a new level. They talk about Jesus, the Church, social justice—when normally they might talk about sports or the weather. Many doubts, fears, and feelings of hope are shared. I think

Rend Your Hearts would make the Lenten season very special to many in our parish."

"It's hard to quarrel with that," said Donna, "but I am concerned how we are going to get the candidates involved. I do think this type of program would be excellent for them. If they participate, they could meet other parishioners, or perhaps be in the same small group as their sponsors. Yet, I am concerned that many of them would not want to commit another weekday evening when they are already coming on Wednesdays."

Then Helen suggested, "We could give them the option of continuing to come on Sunday mornings, but have *Rend Your Hearts* in the place of the Community Hour."

"That could work," said Donna.

"Regardless of when they would come," stated Fr. Stenvic, "what I like about this type of program is that, at least in the liturgical years using the Cycle A Scripture readings, all the people involved in *Rend Your Hearts* will be reading and reflecting on the same readings that form the basis for the scrutinies and for the other Sunday liturgies. Discussing these readings, sharing faith, doing Christian actions, and participating in the prayer service should do a lot toward preparing those involved to really celebrate when they come to the Sunday Masses during Lent."

"I would volunteer to lead the small group on Sunday mornings," said Helen. "I enjoy being with the candidates during the Community Hour, and I would enjoy participating with them and others in one of the *Rend Your Hearts* groups."

At this point Phyllis Johnson told the group that *Rend Your Hearts* had been designed with a special emphasis on raising Catholic consciousness in the area of social justice, and inviting Catholics to become more involved in social justice actions. Phyllis also said that *Rend Your Hearts* could be combined with an Easter-Pentecost program also available from the Washington Archdiocesan Office of Social Development. A group could choose, though, to meet only during Lent or only during the Easter-Pentecost period.

The Core Group ended this part of their meeting by giving the Johnsons the "OK," and asked them to coordinate with the parish council. The group members felt that *Rend Your Hearts* was a natural follow-up to the Community Hour, besides involving a large number of St. Raphael's parishioners in their own *Rend Your Hearts* groups.

THE RITES

About a month after Christmas, Evelyn and her liturgical team began to plan for the liturgical rites that would be celebrated during Lent and Easter—the rite of election, the scrutinies, the presentations, the preparatory rites, and the sacraments of initiation during the Easter Vigil. This was not only going to be their busiest time during the entire initiation journey, but potentially the most rewarding. Their team would plan the liturgies that could be extremely prayerful and memorable for both the candidates and the community. Evelyn knew that these liturgies, especially the Easter Vigil, celebrate the most profound mysteries of the Church's tradition.

The team decided to work hard so that the liturgies would be well coordinated and prayerful. They agreed to meet three times: once before the rite of election, once to plan the scrutinies and the presentations, and once to plan for the preparatory rites and the Easter Vigil liturgy. Fr. Stenvic, as pastor, always met with the team to insure proper coordination. In addition, two of the candidates met with the group to insure that the liturgies would express the thoughts and feelings of those being initiated.

Evelyn brought some helpful resources with her to that first meeting in January:

1. The RCIA, which contains all the liturgies that the team would plan.
2. The lectionary and sacramentary, which contain readings and prayers for the initiation liturgies.
3. "Adult Initiation in the Parish," by Rev. Thomas Welbers (this is Vol. V, No. 1 issue of *Service: Resources for Pastoral Ministry* [Jan.–March 1978], published by Paulist Press, 545 Island Road, Ramsey, New Jersey 07446). This issue has an introduction and suggestions for each of the initiation liturgies from the rite of election through Pentecost.
4. The *National Bulletin on Liturgy*, Vol. 11, No. 64 (May–June 1978), available from Publications Service, 90 Parent Avenue, Ottawa, Ontario, Canada K1N 7B1. This volume presents a

discussion of the initiation rites and offers suggestions for their adaptation.

5. *The Reception of Baptized Christians and the Rite of Baptism during the Easter Vigil* (Washington, D.C.: National Conference of Catholic Bishops, Bishops' Committee on the Liturgy, 1977). This is the actual text of the rites for the celebration of baptism, confirmation, or reception of baptized adults into full communion with the Church during the Easter Vigil. It has been designed as an insert for the sacramentary.

Combining these resources with prayer and a sensitivity to the candidates and parishioners of St. Raphael's, the team prepared meaningful and memorable liturgies during the three times they met.

A week after the Easter Vigil, Evelyn and her team met once again to evaluate and discuss what had occurred. Here are some of their conclusions and reflections on each of the liturgies they prepared.

1. The Rite of Election
   - a practice a week before with the candidates and their godparents made all those involved feel more comfortable, and provided the opportunity to "choreograph" the liturgy.
   - the presence of a bishop at this liturgy created a new sense of pride and community identity.
   - a reception for the bishop, the newly "elect," godparents, candidates for full communion, sponsors and parishioners was an excellent occasion for continuing the rite of election celebration.
   - including prayers and recognition during this rite for those seeking full communion with the Church made these candidates feel welcome and provided yet another occasion to recognize their status as baptized Christians.

2. The Scrutinies
   - these liturgies were well coordinated prayer experiences because a single theme was weaved through the opening prayer, the Scripture readings, the homily, the scrutinies, and the General Intercessions.
   - it was helpful to give the congregation an explanation of the scrutinies before Mass.

- the "elect" and their godparents should be among those processing in with the priest at the beginning of Mass.
- prayers were added so as to remember those seeking full communion with the Church and their sponsors.
- prayers added for the strengthening of the entire community were effective.
- the scrutinies provided an opportunity for a short "testimony" by one of the "elect" on the progress of her journey.
- the second and third scrutinies had to be further adapted in light of the experience of celebrating the first scrutiny.

3. The Presentations of the Creed and the Lord's Prayer
- these liturgies gave a real experience of the community passing on its heritage.
- both liturgies were held in place of a class evening, with sponsors, godparents, and the entire community invited.
- it was helpful to add songs to the liturgies.
- the homily explained the mystery, meaning, and depth of the creed and the Lord's Prayer.
- experiences of both liturgies seemed to be memorable evenings for all who participated.

4. The Preparatory Rites
- a more quiet, prayerful, and reflective period on Holy Saturday afternoon was essential in light of the "busy" Easter Vigil.
- it was important to invite sponsors, spouses and families, and members of the parish.
- music definitely enhanced this liturgy.
- preparatory liturgies were meaningful for those "preparing" to be received into full communion with the Church. The readings and the homily were designed to stress preparation for all the sacraments of initiation—baptism, confirmation, and the eucharist. For example, excerpts from the bishop's homily in the *Rite of Confirmation* were read and meditated on during this Saturday preparatory period.
- this period of waiting, meditation, and prayer was an excellent time for candidates, sponsors, and members of the parish to "testify" to the wonderful works of God that brought them to

this day. It was a time for sharing feelings of thanksgiving and gratitude.

- the time of waiting in the preparatory liturgies was a memorable period of prayer for sponsors, godparents, and members of the parish, especially those who had not experienced this type of liturgy before.

5. The Easter Vigil
   - all members of the liturgical team should work on the coordination of this liturgy so as to make it "flow."
   - the lector or commentator should explain the special features of this Easter Vigil liturgy before the Mass begins. That way everyone will know what to expect and be more open to participate.
   - after the godparents are introduced, it is a good idea for them to present the candidates for baptism (No. 213).
   - the liturgical symbols used at baptism—the font, the white robe (optional), and the candles—should be "big enough" for adults. These symbols should express the reality that is occurring.
   - when there are no candidates for baptism, but only candidates for reception into full communion with the Church, the rite of reception might better be held on Holy Thursday. This would allow for full participation in the Easter triduum.
   - the rite of full reception into the Catholic Church should occur immediately before the baptismal ceremony. Then all the candidates in the class, those newly received into the church and newly baptized, can be confirmed in the same ceremony.
   - since some parishioners are not accustomed to seeing confirmation follow immediately after baptism, the commentator should announce at the appropriate time that this sacrament is occurring.
   - all the priests concelebrating in the rite of confirmation should participate in the laying on of hands.
   - the godparent or sponsor should place his/her right hand on the shoulder of the candidate during the rite of confirmation (No. 231).
   - it was effective for the newly baptized to light the candles of the faithful for renewal of their baptismal promises.

79

- the renewal of baptismal promises was a special moment for those previously nonpracticing Catholics who had made a renewed commitment through attending the catechumenate and Lenten classes.
- all the new Catholics were mentioned by name in the General Intercessions.
- it was a good idea for the new Catholics to receive communion first, with the priest or commentator giving some explanation as to the eucharist being the culmination of their initiation (No. 8). Applause was appropriate at this time since some of the candidates had been waiting months for this moment.
- a party and reception after the Easter Vigil definitely continued the celebration.
- the Easter Vigil liturgy remained a precious memory for all involved, especially the candidates, sponsors, godparents, catechists, and those members of the parish closely associated with the initiation journey.

As the liturgical team completed the evaluation of their liturgies during Lent and the Easter Vigil, Evelyn was emotionally moved. "I never anticipated that these liturgies could be so powerful," she said. "We spent a lot of time planning, but we could only do so much. God must have worked in us and through us. I am wrapped up in wonder. I still don't quite believe it . . . how Larry and some of the others told us about their conversions. I have never experienced anything like it. I don't know what more to say, except, maybe . . . thanks be to God."

THE INTERVIEWS

Let's go back now and join Donna, Tony, and Fr. Stenvic as they continue their interviews with all the candidates during Lent. The three placed special emphasis at this time on the interviews with the baptized candidates and with the previously inactive Catholics. During this period, the baptized candidates would be making a final decision whether to become full members of the Catholic Church. Moreover, Lent could be a time of penance and deepening conversion for those previously inactive Catholics now preparing to renew their baptismal promises with the faithful during the Easter Vigil.

Tony was so pleased with his use of "A Pause along the Journey" in his interviews with the catechumens that he thought he would design a similar type interview form for use with the baptized candidates. Donna and Fr. Stenvic helped him, and they came up with another form of "A Pause along the Journey." Here is what it looked like. (See page 88.) Fr. Stenvic said that the purpose of this form was not to create a strict question-and-answer interview situation, but that it would serve as a guide in dealing with the specific questions and pastoral needs of the candidates.

It turned out that all the candidates, including Maureen and Carol, were received into the Church during the Easter Vigil. They were confirmed and received the eucharist as Catholics for the first time. Larry, Merrill, and the other "elect" were fully initiated into the Church by being baptized, confirmed, and receiving the eucharist. And no longer warranting the label of "nonpracticing," Clarence and the other previously inactive Catholics participated fully in the Easter Vigil liturgy. It was a wonderful evening of prayer and celebration.

About a week after the Easter Vigil, Fr. Stenvic received a phone call from Larry. He was very happy, so he and Paula decided to invite Fr. Stenvic over for dinner. Let's join them in Larry and Paula's dining room.

Larry said, "These last two months have been intense for me . . . well, I guess for all of us. I feel so happy inside. Probably I'm on a 'high' after the Easter Vigil."

"I feel on sort of a 'high' myself," said Fr. Stenvic, "but I would like to hear about some of your experiences, Larry. I have noticed a change in you."

"There has been a lot happening inside," Larry began. "I think that the rite of election was a turning point. Before that time it seemed like I was still sitting on the fence. I would come to Mass with Paula and participate in the other activities of the catechumenate, but I still felt like an outsider looking in. When the bishop asked me if I wanted to receive the sacraments of baptism, confirmation, and the eucharist, I said yes, and I meant it. I was tired of sitting on, the other side. I wanted to be a full member. Then when I wrote my name in the 'book of the elect,' it was like signing my name to a contract to become a member of St. Raphael's. That's what I wanted."

"I recall our conversation on the way home after the rite of election," Paula commented. "You had more of a peace about you."

"That's true," answered Larry, "I had made my decision."

Larry's recalling of his experiences started Paula and Fr. Stenvic to begin thinking about what the last two months had meant to them. The three were feeling very relaxed, and were sipping coffee after dessert.

Fr. Stenvic leaned back in his chair and said, "There has been so much happening during this Lenten season. That Easter Vigil was beautiful . . . but I think the scrutinies were the most powerful experiences for me. I must say, I did like the way those liturgies seemed to 'flow,' from the opening prayer right through the dismissal. I have to give Evelyn a lot of credit for that. But it was the images of Jesus in those liturgies—at the well, healing the man born blind, raising Lazarus from the dead—that were so real to me this year. It was almost like I was there."

"I had some of the same feelings," Larry said, "but my reaction was a little different. In my own mind and heart, I was that blind man reaching out to be healed of my emptiness, and I was Lazarus who needed to be raised to a new life of hope. Yes, I did reach out—I reached out to Jesus and said, 'Heal me! Heal me!' "

The three were silent for a moment, as Paula reached over and took hold of Larry's hand.

"I couldn't help but think of Eric," continued Larry. "He must be with Jesus now, healed and with a new life. I kept thinking about healing and new life as I would read the gospel stories that we heard on those Sunday mornings of the scrutinies. I kept saying to myself, 'Can this really be true?' 'Is a new life possible?' Well, now I know that it is because I feel it inside. I am so thankful."

Paula took back her hand, gave Larry a reassuring glance, and then said, "These past two months have been memorable for me, especially being able to share these experiences with Larry. But it was that time on Saturday afternoon, just before the Easter Vigil, that I will never forget. I was a little squeamish when Larry began to tell his conversion story. I felt embarrassed at first, . . . then I said, 'No!

Don't feel that way, but be thankful because Larry has found something he has been searching for.' When all of us were asked to pray for those about to be baptized, I had such an overwhelming feeling inside. I knew that Larry and I would continue to share on a level that we were never before able to in our marriage."

"This is part of our new life," said Larry softly as he looked toward Paula.

After a time of silence, Fr. Stenvic reflected aloud. "Being the main celebrant at the Easter Vigil was special for me. I can't express what it meant to me as pastor to see all of you 'new Catholics' around that altar during baptism and confirmation, and then to see you come up first to receive the eucharist. I felt like a true pastor. We had spent so much time together over the months, and there you were, no longer called catechumens or candidates, but Catholics. I was proud of you and the people of St. Raphael's."

Then Larry spoke up rather excitedly, "I was so anxious to receive the sacraments and become a full member that I could hardly wait any longer. We kept saying in class '. . . only five more weeks, . . . only four more weeks, . . . only three more weeks. . . . ' Well, it finally came. The highlight of that Vigil ceremony for me was receiving the eucharist for the first time. That made me feel most like a member. When I would go to Mass with Paula, I would sit there while she and the others went up to receive communion. I felt rather alone sitting by myself in the pew, looking at the others go up, and then come back to join me. But at the Easter Vigil, Paula and I and the Armstrongs went up together. I not only received that same Lord who healed the man born blind and raised Lazarus from the dead, but I was able to receive the Lord with friends whom I love. I want to do that every Sunday."

"Richard and Liz Armstrong, Larry's godparents, have been special to us during this time," said Paula. "What impressed me most was the example they presented of a couple who shared their faith deeply—as Larry and I never used to do. We have talked with them about that part of their life, and they gave us some helpful suggestions. They even gave Larry a Bible with both of our names embossed on the cover—Larry and Paula Montgomery. They gave it to us, and a big hug, at the reception after the Easter Vigil."

"We are lucky to have them in the parish," replied Fr. Stenvic.

After relaxing and finishing his second cup of coffee, the priest leaned forward and said to Larry, "I have been enjoying sharing these experiences with you and Paula, but I do have the feeling that all of us are on a 'high.' It is just a week after the Easter Vigil. Although it is good to celebrate, we have to realize that we won't be on 'cloud nine' forever. When you begin to feel low, just remember to be faithful to the daily living of the Christian life that we talked about in the catechumenate, like praying, reading the Scriptures, and so on."

"I am thankful for this time," Larry said, "but you are right that the bubble may burst. However, I am convinced now that there is good news, and that my emptiness can become fullness. I have experienced this over the past year and a half with Paula and the community at St. Raphael's. In a way, through Eric's death, I have been given a new life. There is still a hole in my heart when I think about Eric, but I am hopeful that someday it will be completely filled."

As Fr. Stenvic was driving home that evening, he was feeling very prayerful. The time with Paula and Larry had been wonderful. He thought, "How can God be so good to me." Then, as the image of the confirmation ceremony during the Easter Vigil flashed in front of him, Fr. Stenvic smiled. Larry, Maureen, Carol . . . all of them standing in front of the altar. There they were, the "new Catholics"—the fruit of the evangelization and initiation programs that the community at St. Raphael's had planned and carried out. "Thanks be to God," he said. "Thanks be to God."

As he drove into the rectory driveway, Fr. Stenvic was eager to attend the next meeting of the Core Group and see how the period of postbaptismal catechesis was progressing. This was the final period of the RCIA at St. Raphael's . . . at least for this year.

FOURTH SUNDAY OF LENT

Justice must be pursued with the help of Christ the Light. "Not as man sees does God see, because man sees the appearance, but the Lord looks into the heart" (first reading). The second reading urges us to "live as children of light. Light produces every kind of goodness and justice and truth." The third reading indicates the necessity of "spiritual sight" which must come from Christ, the Light—"I came into the world to make the sightless see." (1 Samuel 16:1,6–7,10–13 Ephesians 5:8–14 John 9:1–41)

Faith Sharing
Christ repeatedly condemned failure to see, hear, and understand. The power of the Gospel enables Christians to be open to the world and to perceive it as God does.

1. How would you make an important choice in your life? Who would share in the process of decision-making and to what extent? St. Paul urges the Ephesians to "be correct in your judgment of what pleases the Lord." What informs and guides such a judgment? Have you ever experienced a kind of spiritual blindness? Why? How did you come to sight?
2. Why were the blind man's "neighbors and the people who had been accustomed to seeing him begging" and the pharisees so reluctant to believe that he had been healed? Are there areas in which you are resistant to new truth, where it would be too costly for you to find out that you're wrong? Why? Are there people from whom you're not willing to learn?
3. Jesus spoke often of bringing division. What did he mean? Have you ever experienced this?
4. As in last week's Gospel, again this week Jesus reveals his identity directly. Why did he do so? What was the response to his revelation?

Action Suggestions
Three weeks of Lent have passed. Are you satisfied with your efforts to change and become "new" again? Spend some reflective time this week in educating yourself.

1. Read *Food First,* Lappé and Collins.
2. Join Bread for the World, a Christian citizens advocacy group working to alleviate hunger and its causes. Monthly newsletters are sent to members informing them of needed action. Send $10 to Bread for the World, 207 East 16th Street, New York, N.Y. 10003.
3. Have everyone in your prayer community or family clip one news article this week which describes an injustice. Talk about the article with a friend.
4. Organize an evening of "Education to Justice" in your parish.

5. Order the following documents from the United States Catholic Conference for your reading and reflection:

Peace on Earth, Pope John XXIII
On the Development of Peoples, Pope Paul VI
Justice in the World, 1971 Synod of Bishops

United States Catholic Conference, 1312 Massachusetts Ave., NW, Washington, D.C. 20005 (202-659-6640).

6. Add a candle to your "waiting table" as a sign of Christ's presence in your life. If you can, make your own white candle and decorate it with Easter symbols. Cut a cross in the center and paint it with nail polish. At the points of the cross and in its center, pierce the candle with a hot skewer and insert five cloves (symbols of Christ's wounds). At the top of the candle draw an alpha and at the bottom an omega (symbols of Christ, the beginning and the end). Print the year on the candle. Light the candle during the Easter season.

Prayer
(Preparation: a small table . . . on the table, a large candle, lit; a smaller candle at each person's place, unlit)

We adore you, O Christ, and we bless you.
  FOR BY YOUR HOLY CROSS YOU HAVE REDEEMED THE
    WORLD.
O Lord, open my lips.
  AND MY MOUTH SHALL DECLARE YOUR PRAISE.

Opening Song

"This Little Light" (or some other appropriate song or recording)

Psalm 23

The Lord is my shepherd;
  I have everything I need.
He lets me rest in fields of green grass
  and leads me to quiet pools of fresh water.
He gives me new strength.

He guides me in the right way,
  as he has promised.
Even if that way goes through deepest
    darkness
  I will not be afraid, Lord,
  because you are with me!
Your shepherd's rod and staff keep me safe.

You prepare a banquet for me,
  where all my enemies can see me;

you welcome me by pouring ointment on my head
    and filling my cup to the brim.
Certainly your goodness and love will be
        with me as long as I live;
    and your house will be my home forever.

Reading
Matthew 11:1–6

Silence and Shared Prayer
(This prayer is concluded by lighting the individual candles from the large
candle and reciting the Beatitudes together)

Happy are you poor: the Kingdom of God is yours!
Happy are you who are hungry now: you will be filled!
Happy are you who weep now: you will laugh!
Happy are you when people hate you, and reject you and insult
        you, and say that you are evil because of the Son of Man!
Be happy when that happens and dance for joy, for a great reward
        is kept for you in heaven.
But how terrible for you who are rich now: you have had your
        easy life!
How terrible for you who are full now: you will go hungry!
How terrible for you who laugh now: you will mourn and weep!
How terrible when all speak well of you; for their ancestors said the very
        same things to the false prophets.

ST. RAPHAEL'S PARISH
A PAUSE ALONG THE JOURNEY

Since October we have walked along the path toward your being received into full communion with the Catholic Church at St. Raphael's parish. We want to pause now and reflect on our journey up to this point. The following questions should be helpful.

1. Do you feel that you are continuing your conversion to Christ and experiencing a new way of life in the Catholic Church?

2. Do you have a deeper understanding of God's love for you and of his loving plan of salvation in which you share? Are you beginning to see how this love is expressed through your participation in the Catholic community of St. Raphael's parish.

3. Do you feel concerned or puzzled about any teachings of the Catholic Church?

4. The Catholic faith is a way of life, a new way of living. Do you feel that you have a growing desire to:
   a. pray and read Scripture?
   b. live your faith such that you expect to experience God's love for you, and allow the Holy Spirit to lead you in living the Catholic faith?
   c. exercise charity toward your neighbor, even to the point of self-renunciation?
   d. live according to Catholic moral teaching?

5. Do you feel a growing yearning to spread the gospel and become involved in various areas of service within the Catholic Church?

6. Do you have any questions about your participation in the Mass, or in other liturgical rites of the Catholic Church?

7. Do you have a supportive relationship with your sponsor?

8. Do you want another person or family, other than your present sponsor, to be your sponsor at confirmation?

9. Do you feel a new identity developing within yourself, an identity as a Catholic?

10. Do you wish to come into full communion with the Catholic Church and receive confirmation and the eucharist during the Easter Vigil?

Note: You may wish to discuss these questions with your sponsors. We on the pastoral team may also be talking with your sponsors to seek their opinion on how you are progressing along your journey.

Chapter Five

POSTBAPTISMAL CATECHESIS

Our journey is coming to an end. We have travelled a long distance through the previous periods and stages of the RCIA, to arrive at the period of postbaptismal catechesis from Easter to Pentecost, the final period of our initiation journey. We shall approach postbaptismal catechesis in the same way that we have approached previous chapters. First, we shall look at the guidelines and suggestions of the RCIA. Then, we shall see what this period might look like in a parish.

POSTBAPTISMAL CATECHESIS IN THE RCIA

A Core Group seeking guidelines within the RCIA for postbaptismal catechesis will find some clear and challenging paragraphs, but the guidelines presented can be read in a matter of minutes. In many ways, this period of the RCIA is similar to that of evangelization and precatechumenate. General guidelines are given, but there is little within the RCIA itself that communities can draw upon to make these periods of the rite come alive within the parish. We come to the same conclusion here as we did in our discussion of the period of evangelization and precatechumenate: Those in a parish responsible for postbaptismal catechesis will need to understand the few guidelines presented, and then creatively develop programs that meet the particular needs and situation of the parish.

There are some key paragraphs within the RCIA that give the intent and goal of postbaptismal catechesis. No. 37 talks about this period between Easter and Pentecost as a time when both the neophytes (new Catholics) and the community immerse themselves more deeply in the death and resurrection of Jesus which they celebrated at the Easter Vigil. This is accomplished through participating in the eucharist, reading the Scriptures, and by doing works of charity. During this period the neophytes are to reflect on their experience of receiving the sacraments of initiation (No. 38). They are also to continue growing in the Christian life through attending a special neophyte Mass with their sponsors and others from the community during the Sundays from Easter to Pentecost (Nos. 39–40). The neophytes are to experience the fact that they are part of a Catholic community that has the eucharist at the center of its life.

The RCIA stresses that the community give continued pastoral care to its new members during the period of postbaptismal catechesis. Parishioners, sponsors and godparents, and pastors must try to encourage the new Catholics to participate fully in the life of the community (No. 235). This same type of pastoral care is to be given to the new Catholics, previously baptized, but now in full communion with the Catholic Church (No. 305).

POSTBAPTISMAL CATECHESIS IN THE PARISH

From the guidelines presented, what might the period of postbaptismal catechesis look like in a parish? Well, . . . let's join our friends at St. Raphael's as they plan for this final period of the RCIA. We shall join them at a Core Group meeting shortly after the rite of election. Previous to the meeting, Helen, Fr. Stenvic, Tony, and Donna had volunteered to design a coordinated plan for the period of postbaptismal catechesis and to present this at the Core Group meeting.

Fr. Stenvic is the first to speak. "The four of us have had a rewarding time meeting together, and we feel we have a plan that will meet most of our needs. Since what we are presenting is new to you, please hold your comments until the four of us give you our report, and then we can discuss it as a group."

Fr. Stenvic's suggestion was agreeable to the members, so he continued. "We received most of the inspiration for our plan from No. 37 of the RCIA. Our entire community here at St. Raphael's, including our new Catholics, is to meditate on the Gospel, participate in the eucharist, and perform works of charity during this time from Easter to Pentecost. The RCIA argues that if we do this, we should experience more of the dying and rising with Christ in our personal lives and as a community."

"As the four of us were talking," said Fr. Stenvic, "paragraph No. 37 began to make sense in a very concrete way. Let me explain. The time from Easter to Pentecost is also known as the 'great Sunday,' the special 50-day period each year when the Church celebrates the resurrection of Jesus. We prepare for 40 days during Lent, and then celebrate the resurrection for another 50 days until Pentecost. The Scripture lessons for each Sunday, as well as the prayers said during Mass, give us much of the meaning of this 50-day period. After reading these Scripture lessons and prayers, the four of us came to the conclusion that the time from Easter to Pentecost celebrates who we are as the Christian community of St. Raphael's. The readings and prayers speak about community living, the eucharist, and doing works of charity. This is very similar to No. 37 of the RCIA."

"What we are proposing to you," continued Fr. Stenvic, "is that we truly celebrate this 50-day period at St. Raphael's. We want to do this by involving the entire community in celebrating the eucharist, by encouraging our parishioners to get involved in Christian sub-groups of our community, and by doing works of charity. By emphasizing these three areas, we feel that we will not only be planning something meaningful for the parish, but will also be providing the best pastoral care for our new members."

At this point Fr. Stenvic was very enthusiastic, but he noticed some blank stares on a few of the faces. So he said, "I think I need to be more specific. I'm afraid that I am losing some of you in this more abstract type of presentation. Well, we are prepared to be specific. I will begin by talking about the planning for our eucharistic celebrations from Easter to Pentecost. Then, Helen will tell you about our plan to encourage smaller Christian support communities; Tony will tell you about our Christian service program; and Donna will give you a few ideas about our plan of pastoral care for our new Catholics. We feel that our Core Group's effort in this phase of the RCIA should be as strong and consistent as it has been in the other phases.

We have worked hard to have a rather complete catechumenate and period of illumination. We would like to have a period of postbaptismal catechesis on a par with these others."

Then Fr. Stenvic spoke briefly about the celebrations of the eucharist. "Some of the Scripture lessons read at the Sunday Masses during this 50-day period speak about the importance of the eucharist. These readings would provide the basis for me to preach on how the eucharist is so central to our lives here at St. Raphael's. We gather each Sunday to remember how we are a part of Jesus' dying and rising. Of course, our special Mass at 10:00 on Sunday will be tailored to help the new Catholics reflect on the meaning of their participation in the eucharist, and their continuing to die and rise with Christ. As we celebrate the Sunday liturgies, hear the Scriptures read, and listen to the prayers and homilies during this 50-day period, we should realize more clearly who we are as a church living the life of the resurrected Jesus."

At this point, it was Helen's turn to speak to the Core Group. She asked if there were any questions concerning their report so far, but the group wanted to wait until the complete plan was presented.

Then Helen said, "I am pleased to be a member of this planning group. Fr. Stenvic mentioned that our proposed emphasis on smaller, more supportive groups comes right out of the Scripture readings for this 50-day period. Acts 2, for example, talks about Christians living together in community. From my experience, I am convinced that many members of St. Raphael's community deepen their Christian lives as they participate in smaller Christian groups. Some members from Cursillo meet together during the week, as do some of the people from our charismatic prayer group. They seem to find value in this. We also have a large number of parishioners involved at the present time in the Lenten *Rend Your Hearts* groups."

Helen could see that there was interest, so she continued. "What we want to do during this 50-day period after Easter is emphasize the benefit of these small Christian groups, and invite parishioners who are not involved to commit themselves to one of these groups from Easter to Pentecost. I mentioned at a previous Core Group meeting that the Archdiocesan Office of Social Development of Washington, D.C., had designed a program for Easter-Pentecost very similar to their *Rend Your Hearts* program. It is called *Jesus Is Lord* and has the same format as the Lenten program except that the focus is on the Easter-Pentecost period. I propose that we make that program available at St. Raphael's this year. There may be some from the *Rend Your Hearts* groups who wish to be with the same group from Lent to Pentecost. Others may wish to sign up only for the period after Easter."

"Since we will be emphasizing the importance of small Christian support groups," Helen said, "we will also be encouraging those in organizations of the parish to meet and use the *Jesus Is Lord* format. That way, just as in *Rend Your Hearts,* many of our parishioners will have read the Sunday readings in their groups and be better prepared to celebrate the eucharist with the larger community on Sunday morning."

The group was listening intently. Many of the Core Group members had experienced the benefits of growing in the Christian life through small group activity. They were convinced that this experience should be offered to more of the parishioners of St. Raphael's. This is why they liked what Helen was saying.

Helen continued, "What I am emphasizing is that the 50-day period from Easter to Pentecost will be a time when we as a parish can experience the importance of Christian community, not only as we worship together on Sunday, but as we meet in our smaller communities during the week. Moreover, some who experience these small groups during Lent and Easter may want to continue after Pentecost. Some could meet together for different reasons such as reading the spiritual masters, organizing around social justice issues, taking care of the elderly, or supporting our youth ministry program. These groups could meet once or twice a month and make commitments to one another. Some of our new Catholics should be encouraged to continue in one of these smaller groups."

At this point, Fr. Stenvic spoke up. "I don't want to interrupt what you are saying, Helen, but I'm sure that the others here would be interested in knowing about the *Koinonia Handbook* developed at the Paulist Center Community [5 Park Street, Boston, Mass. 02108]. When you first showed me this handbook, I was impressed. For those of you on the Core Group not familiar with this word, *koinonia* is a Greek term used to describe these smaller Christian groups that we have been talking about. The *Koinonia Handbook* gives some

93

excellent suggestions concerning how such small groups can grow and prosper in a parish; it also explains how the larger parish is enriched as these group members come to worship at the Sunday liturgies."

"What Helen and Fr. Stenvic said has reinforced my conviction that these smaller Christian groups can be the basis for works of charity in our parish," remarked Tony. "I will be giving you more on this later, but I think it would be excellent if the group that visits the Holy Family nursing home could meet and pray together, as well as do their visitations each week. Sometimes they get discouraged. They need the support of one another."

"You seem to be stealing my fire," retorted Helen, "but that is OK. If you are enthused about this small group Christian community approach during the 50 days after Easter, I will see if I can get two coordinators. The Johnsons have found coordinating the *Rend Your Hearts* program to be challenging and rewarding, and others in our parish may want to coordinate the *Jesus Is Lord* program from Easter to Pentecost."

Then Fr. Stenvic spoke. "Thanks, Helen, for telling us about the small group component of our plan for postbaptismal catechesis at St. Raphael's. As I mentioned earlier, the Scripture readings and the prayers of the liturgy for this 50-day period bring to light that a Church must be active in doing works of justice and charity. Tony has prepared a report on this part of our Easter-Pentecost plan."

After shuffling some of his papers, Tony began. "Just as Helen has been talking about helping our parishioners experience who they are as the People of God by getting involved in small groups from Easter to Pentecost, I too want to get more people involved in doing works of charity during this period. Each of us renewed our baptismal promises during the Easter Vigil. We all recognized in that liturgy that it was through baptism that we entered into the dying and rising of Jesus. Our baptism also gave us the commission to carry on the saving work of Jesus through doing works of justice and charity."

"I think you need to be more concrete," interrupted Donna. "How do you propose to help us experience what we supposedly promised during the Easter Vigil?"

"What I am proposing," Tony explained, "is that we have two

Sundays during this Easter-Pentecost period in which we would emphasize the importance of Christian service and doing works of charity. Again, the emphasis on Christian service comes right out of the Scripture readings and the liturgical prayers for the Sundays during the 50-day Easter-Pentecost period. On one Sunday, through the homily, we would invite all the parishioners to become more aware of their Christian responsibility to do works of service. After the homily, we would pass out 'need' cards and ask our parishioners to identify people and areas in need. Some may feel, for example, that we need to support the ministry at the jail, as that facility lies within our parish boundaries. Two or three weeks later we would have another Sunday where we would ask our parishioners to respond to some of these needs which were identified earlier."

"This would require a lot of work," commented Evelyn, who had been listening silently up to this time.

" It would," replied Tony, "but I have talked with some volunteers who would coordinate this Christian service program. They are committed to spend the time. There are, however, two more phases of this program that I want to tell you about. One phase involves Pentecost Sunday. The Scriptures and prayers for this Sunday speak about Christians going forth in the power of the Holy Spirit. I would like to see us have a short commissioning ceremony at one of the Masses on Pentecost for those who responded to meet the needs that we identified during the Easter-Pentecost period. Then, following Pentecost, there would be training for those who volunteered, as well as planning for ways to carry out this particular form of Christian service. I know it would take a lot of time, but we are prepared to make that kind of commitment."

"One thing I like about what you are saying," reflected Donna, "is that this would give us a chance to talk to the new Catholics more about the meaning of Christian service, and the type of service to which they might specifically commit themselves."

"That's true," said Helen, "but I can also see a connection between what Tony is presenting and what I have said concerning the smaller Christian communities. It could happen that a group meeting in the *Jesus Is Lord* program would decide to sign up to meet a specific need that was identified. For example, I could see one of the groups volunteering to assist in the jail ministry of our parish."

"Also," commented Evelyn, "Pentecost would be an excellent time to 'commission' those volunteering for these new forms of Christian service."

"I thought we weren't going to have any discussion until we finished presenting our report." said Fr. Stenvic. "But it sounds as if you are already seeing a pattern concerning how our Easter-Pentecost plan emphasizes who we are as a Church here at St. Raphael's. I want to point out again that it would be at the Sunday eucharist when we would come together and celebrate our unity as members of this community.

"Not only that," said Evelyn sponteneously, "but we should realize that the Easter-Pentecost period occurs each year. If we would repeat our emphasis on eucharist, small Christian communities, and Christian service each year, soon our parishioners would begin to take this time period as seriously as they do the 40 days of Lent. Our parishioners eventually should come to realize that Lent and the time from Easter to Pentecost should be considered as one period of time—first we lead up to the Easter Vigil, and then we celebrate the resurrection for 50 days afterwards."

"That's a good point," replied Fr. Stenvic. "While it would take a few years to develop that consciousness at St. Raphael's, it is a consciousness that would benefit all of us."

"I'm concerned," interrupted Donna, "that we might be forgetting our new Catholics in this larger discussion about Easter-Pentecost. So, let me give you the plan that Fr. Stenvic, Tony, Helen, and I discussed. We have consulted with Larry and Maureen, so what we are presenting would seem to meet the needs of many of our potential new Catholics. As you know from No. 37 of the RCIA, postbaptismal catechesis is a time for both the new Catholics and the community to participate in the eucharist, read the Scriptures, and perform works of justice and charity. There are no classes for the new Catholics, since their new 'classroom' is celebrating the Sunday eucharist with us. We are proposing to continue the special neophyte Mass at 10:00, just as we had it throughout their period of formation."

Donna continued, "Fr. Stenvic has decided to use the Sunday readings from Cycle A (RCIA, No. 40), so that he can instruct the neophytes who will be attending that Mass with their sponsors and godparents. We need to insure that our coordinator of publicity informs the parishioners that the 10:00 Mass is for the new Catholics. I think our parishioners will be delighted to discover the talents and gifts of people like Larry, Maureen, and Carol as they become active in our community."

"However," said Donna, "after we talked with Larry and Maureen, and discussed the pastoral needs of the new Catholics, we felt that more was required than just having them come to the 10:00 Mass. We are proposing that they continue to meet as a group after this Mass on the Sundays from Easter to Pentecost. Their sponsors and godparents would also be invited, as would any of the parishioners interested in attending. You see, the new Catholics have developed a strong community over the months they have been together in the catechumenate and during the period of illumination. As they continue to meet, they should have a lot to share about their experiences of the Easter Vigil and what being new Catholics means to them. Having them meet as a group after the 10:00 Mass would also allow us to help them reflect more deeply on their experience of receiving the sacraments and living the Catholic way of life."

The Core Group liked Donna's plan. She went on, "In addition to spending that time after the 10:00 Mass reflecting on their new status as Catholics, we are proposing that we use the *Jesus Is Lord* program at that time and adapt it to our needs. The format of this program would help us focus on the Sunday readings. We realize, though, that we could only use the *Jesus Is Lord* format for the Cycle A readings because Fr. Stenvic will be using these readings at the 10:00 Mass for those newly baptized or received into the Church. Meeting together would also give us an opportunity to continue to discuss the meaning of Christian service with the new Catholics, and help them make a commitment to some type of service, if they have not done so already."

"I do like the idea of having the new Catholics meet after Mass," commented Evelyn, "but you need to insure that they play an active part in determining what your group will do during those meetings."

"We have been trying to include them in our planning all along," replied Donna. After she paused for a moment and looked at her notes, Donna said, "There are a couple of things that I failed to

97

mention. No. 327 of the RCIA speaks about some form of celebration to close the period of initiation. We propose having this on Pentecost. Not only could we have a special ceremony of blessing and thanksgiving for the new Catholics, but we could commission them to carry out the roles of Christian service that they have chosen. This would coincide with Tony's program emphasizing Christian service during the 50-day period and the commissioning on Pentecost Sunday."

"That has real possibilities," said Fr. Stenvic, "and it seems consistent with the types of things we have done throughout the initiation process. We need to insure, though, that we have someone to coordinate this program after the 10:00 Mass and to see that the new Catholics continue to be integrated into the life of our community after Pentecost."

"I would like to volunteer to do that," replied Donna. "I have been working with these people since October and I know them well. I could get one of the neophytes to help me."

"That would be great," said Fr. Stenvic. "Well, the four of us have presented our plan for the period of postbaptismal catechesis at St. Raphael's. We have tried to consider the community as well as the needs of the new Catholics. What do you think?"

After some discussion, Evelyn spoke up, expressing the feelings of many in the group. "I think your plan is sound. We should try it. There are many details to be worked out, but the general framework of your plan definitely would help the people of St. Raphael's celebrate the 50-day period from Easter-Pentecost, as well as meet the pastoral and catechetical needs of the new Catholics. Having an emphasis on the eucharist, small Christian groups, and on works of justice and charity would help us to experience who we are as a Church celebrating this 50-day period of Jesus' resurrection. Your plan would also give us a basis for continuing to live as a Christian community after Pentecost."

The meeting ended with the Core Group adopting the plan given by Fr. Stenvic, Donna, Helen, and Tony for the period of postbaptismal catechesis at St. Raphael's.

Chapter Six

HOPE FOR THE FUTURE

Welcome home, or welcome to a new beginning. We have ended our journey through the periods and stages of the RCIA. Let's look back over our roadmap and see where we have travelled and stopped along the way:

evangelization and precatechumenate	period 1
rite of becoming catechumens	stage 1
catechumenate	period 2
rite of election (First Sunday of Lent)	stage 2
illumination (during Lent)	period 3
sacraments of initiation (Easter Vigil)	stage 3
postbaptismal catechesis (Easter-Pentecost)	period 4

Let's also look again at a possible time sequence for our journey:

June:
> Core Group plans for the RCIA

July—August:
> Planning for the evangelization program, and planning for the precatechumenate and catechumenate

September—October
> Evangelization, and sponsor selection and training

October—November:
> Precatechumenate

November—February:
> Rite of Becoming Catechumens and catechumenate

First Sunday of Lent:
> Rite of Election and the beginning of purification and enlightenment

Third Sunday of Lent—Fourth Sunday of Lent—Fifth Sunday of Lent:
> Scrutinies

Easter Vigil:
> Sacraments of initiation—baptism, confirmation, and eucharist

Easter—Pentecost:
> Postbaptismal catechesis

Pentecost:
> Celebrates the ending of one evangelization and initiation cycle

May—June:
> Core Group evaluates the RCIA

Unlike some roadmaps, the one we used does not go out of date. The directions for the different periods and stages of the journey may become clearer and more understandable, but the map itself remains the same. It is used year after year as a parish community travels the journey up to the Easter Vigil, and then concentrates on living the Christian life centered in the eucharist. As the RCIA "recycles" in a parish year after year, parishioners will become more accustomed to travelling along the journey indicated in the periods and stages of the rite. Each year there would be an evaluation, each year a renewed effort to travel along the evangelization and initiation journey with greater confidence and trust. Travelling within the paschal mystery definitely can be a purifying adult journey into the fullness of Christ and his Church.

RCIA IN THE PARISH

Let's join our friends in the Core Group at St. Raphael's for one last time. It is now early June and the period of postbaptismal catechesis and Pentecost is over for this year. As we join the group, they are discussing parts of their journey through the RCIA and making plans for next year. Fr. Stenvic is first to speak.

"Before we begin, let me introduce someone whom all of you have met—Larry Montgomery. As you probably know, Larry was in my small group through the catechumenate and period of illumination. He and I have had a number of rewarding talks together over the past year. When Larry and I had our final interview before Pentecost, we were discussing how he might become more active in the parish, especially how he could use his gifts and talents to serve others. Well, . . . Larry, why don't you tell your own story?"

Then Larry sat up in his chair and began. "The more I became committed to the Catholic way of life at St. Raphael's, the more I wanted to get involved and help others in the same way that I have been loved and helped. When we were discussing the different types of Christian service during our *Jesus Is Lord* group after Easter, Donna mentioned that one of the needs of the parish was to have people assist her in the office of catechist next year. I didn't commit myself at the time, but I did go home and talk with Paula. She thought I had gifts and talents in this area. I definitely appreciated the way Donna and the others cared for me, especially during our Wednesday evening classes. Now I want to extend that same kind of love to others."

Then Fr. Stenvic spoke. "Donna, Tony, and I are pleased with the possibility of Larry assisting Donna on our catechetical team. Larry worked very well with us when we met as a team during the catechumenate and the period of illumination, and we would like to see him as an assistant next year. He normally will not be coming to our Core Group meetings, but we invited him today to help us evaluate the evangelization and initiation programs we had this year. Perhaps, too, he can give us some helpful suggestions as we plan to implement the RCIA next year."

"We're glad to have you with us, Larry," said Evelyn.

After Larry was introduced, the Core Group spent a long time evaluating the different periods and stages of the RCIA as they had been experienced at St. Raphael's. They had passed out questionnaires to evaluate the *Rend Your Hearts* and the *Jesus Is Lord* programs. Through their surveys, interviews with the new Catholics, and talks with a number of the parishioners the Core Group felt they had adequate data to evaluate their programs and to begin planning for evangelization and initiation at St. Raphael's next year.

After some hesitation, Donna spoke up. "Before we begin our planning, there is something I would like to share with you. Sometimes it's hard to talk about feelings openly, but I want all of you to know how valuable it has been for me to work with you this year as a Core Group member. I was rather skeptical about my own involvement when I first joined the team. I really didn't feel 'holy,' or that I was that well trained to be a catechist for these adults. I had many doubts and fears. But I guess that Fr. Stenvic had faith in me. The times that we prayed together on our team meant a lot, and I began to realize that God had a powerful hand in all of this, and that I could do only so much."

After a moment of silence, Donna continued. "I think it was during Lent that I began to experience more of a change in myself. I developed more faith, or trusted in God more ... I really don't know. But I do know that after participating in the scrutinies and the presentations, I came to that Easter Vigil with a changed heart myself. I was so convinced that what I was doing was right. We were forming these candidates to be Christians. I came to realize that I grew more deeply as a Christian in the process of working with Larry and the others. This wasn't so obvious to me that I could say, 'I'm becoming holier' or anything like that; yet I did have the awareness that I was being drawn closer to God. That is why I am so thankful for being a member of this Core Group. Each one of you had a part in bringing me closer to God—and that's true for you, too, Larry, and the rest of the new Catholics."

After Donna spoke, the others began to talk about what being on the Core Group meant to them. Then Tony said, "I think that all of us who have gone through a year of the RCIA have experienced something precious. We have travelled along a journey of conversion and growth ourselves. I definitely want to do the RCIA again next year. Moreover, the evaluation interviews and data show that our parishioners would like to see the RCIA implemented again."

As the Core Group continued their meeting, developing their general plan for each of the periods and stages of the RCIA, there was a feeling of peace and excitement among the group members. They knew that there would be a certain amount of confusion and difficulty, just as there has been the past year. But there was the feeling of hope. The Core Group members had the sense that somehow the Lord was working mightily in their midst.

BIBLIOGRAPHY

Becoming a Catholic Christian. New York: William H. Sadlier, Inc., 1978.

Bohr, David. *Evangelization in America.* New York: Paulist Press, 1977.

Clark, Stephen B. *Building Christian Communities.* Notre Dame, Ind.: Ave Maria Press, 1972.

Finding New Life in the Spirit. Notre Dame, Ind.: Charismatic Renewal Services, Inc., 1972.

Jesus Is Lord. Washington, D.C.: Office of Social Development of the Archdiocese of Washington, D.C., 1977.

Kavanagh, Aidan. *The Shape of Baptism: The Rite of Christian Initiation.* New York: Pueblo Publishing Company, 1978.

Kieran, Rev. Richard A. *Parish Evangelization Planning Guide.* Distributed by the Paulist Office for Evangelization, Washington, D.C.

Koinonia Handbook. Boston: Paulist Center Community, 1977.

Liturgy, Vol. 22, No. 1 (January 1977).

Made, Not Born, New Perspectives on Christian Initiation and the Catechumenate. Notre Dame, Ind.: University of Notre Dame Press, 1976.

National Bulletin on Liturgy, Vol. 11, No. 64 (May–June 1978).

Pope Paul VI. *On Evangelization in the Modern World.* Washington, D.C.: United States Catholic Conference Publications Office, 1976.

Rend Your Hearts. Washington, D.C.: Office of Social Development of the Archdiocese of Washington, D.C., 1977.

Rite of Christian Initiation of Adults. Washington, D.C.: United States Catholic Conference Publication Office, 1974.

Rite of Reception of Baptized Christians into Full Communion with the Catholic Church. Washington, D.C.: United States Catholic Conference Publication Office, 1976.

The Life in the Spirit Seminars. Notre Dame, Ind.: Charismatic Renewal Services, Inc., 1973.

The Reception of Baptized Christians and the Rite of Baptism during the Easter Vigil. Washington, D.C.: National Conference of Catholic Bishops, Bishops' Committee on the Liturgy, 1977.

The St. Bernadette's Evangelism Experiment. Washington, D.C.: The Paulist Office for Evangelization, 1977.

The Unchurched American. Princeton, N.J.: The Princeton Religion Research Center and the Gallup Organization, Inc., 1978.

We Care/We Share. Washington, D.C.: The Paulist Office for Evangelization, 1976.

Welbers, Rev. Thomas. "Adult Initiation in the Parish." *Service: Resources for Pastoral Ministry,* Vol. V., No. 1 (January–March 1978).